HELPING STUDENTS REMEMBER

EXERCISES AND STRATEGIES TO STRENGTHEN MEMORY

MILTON J. DEHN

WILEY

John Wiley & Sons. Inc.

Library of Congress Cataloging-in-Publication Data:

ISBN 978-0-470-91997-2 (pbk)
ISBN 978-1-118-11789-7 (ebk)
ISBN 978-1-118-11791-0 (ebk)
ISBN 978-1-118-11790-3 (ebk)

Printed in the United States of America

10 9 8 7 6 5 4 3 2 1

Dedicated to the memory of my maternal grandfather, Ralph J. Lahn, who was born in 1898. Many of the wonderful stories he told me when I was a child are still stored in my memory.

Contents

Lower Level Workbook

Upper Level Workbook

Appendixes

Acknowledgments

I wish to thank the following for their suggestions and editing:
Danielle M. Brown, Saukville School District, Saukville, Wisconsin
Benjamin Burns, Tomah School District, Tomah, Wisconsin
Paula A. Dehn, Schoolhouse Educational Services, Onalaska, Wisconsin.

Introduction

The memory training program in this workbook consists of evidence-based exercises and strategies designed to enhance memory in children and adolescents. The workbook is divided into two levels: the lower level, for children in grades 3 through 6, and the upper level, for youth in grades 7 through 12. The upper level program is also suitable for college students with learning disabilities and memory impairments. Although the program can be used effectively with small groups of students, it is mainly intended for one-on-one instruction. You, the *trainer*, should familiarize yourself with the entire set of directions for the level you intend to use before you begin working with a student. It is not necessary for the student to practice every exercise or learn every strategy in the workbook, but the lessons are arranged in a sequence that would facilitate using the entire program. To achieve measureable results, you should work with the student a minimum of eight weeks, with sessions totaling at least two hours per week.

This workbook is a follow-up to the book, *Long-Term Memory Problems in Children and Adolescents: Assessment, Intervention, and Effective Instruction* (Dehn, 2010). The book provides additional details on the methods in this workbook, including the rationale and the research base for the methods. Dehn's 2010 text also covers details on different long-term memory systems, memory impairments, the neuropsychological basis of memory, selective cross-battery assessment of memory, risk factors for memory impairments, and effective classroom instruction for memory problems. Also, some of the exercises and interventions for short-term and working memory problems found in this workbook are discussed in *Working Memory and Academic Learning: Assessment and Intervention* (Dehn, 2008). See the References section of this workbook for additional recommended resources (e.g., Alloway & Gathercole, 2006; Baddeley, 1986) on working memory problems and interventions.

The main purpose of this workbook is to help students whose academic learning is suffering because of a memory deficit or because they have not learned to effectively utilize their memory capabilities. The focus of this workbook is on the creation of lasting memories for the factual material students are required to learn in school. Of course, students without identified memory problems will also benefit from completing the training in this workbook. Regardless of the student's memory abilities, what he or she learns from this workbook will do him or her no harm.

After training in, sufficient practice with, and application of the methods included in this workbook, most students should improve their retention and recall of the academic material they are trying to commit to memory. Additional results should include a greater understanding of how memory works, acquisition of several new memory strategies, and an improved ability to independently select and apply effective memory strategies to a variety of memory challenges. Which of these outcomes are actually achieved depends on the characteristics of the student and how faithfully the training methods are implemented. One of the foremost determining factors is the extent of practice. For maintenance and generalization of memory strategies to occur, there needs to be sufficient practice (see Appendix A). Younger students will require more guided practice than older students, provided the older students make an effort to apply the strategies to their academic studies. For the exercises designed to improve working memory performance, there can be no brain-based changes unless there is regular and extensive practice at levels that challenge the student.

Although children and adolescents with severe memory impairments, such as those with ongoing amnesia from a severe head injury, will benefit from this training program, some of the methods may not be effective for them (Cohen & Conway, 2008; Squire & Schacter, 2002). Such students may need more training geared specifically toward "everyday" memory problems encountered in daily living (see Wilson, 2009 for advice). On the other hand, students with mild to moderate memory problems are likely to benefit from nearly all aspects of this training program.

Trainers' Qualifications

The primary intended trainers for this program are teachers and psychologists. Although regular education teachers could apply some of the approaches on a classroom-wide basis, memory training of students will usually fall upon those who have time to conduct small group or individual sessions. Thus, special education teachers, school psychologists, and counselors are likely to be the most frequent users of these materials. Psychologists, tutors, and other professionals working with youth outside of schools will also find these materials useful, but in such instances it is important to connect the training with the student's current academic coursework. A background in psychology and special education is helpful, but not required. What is essential is that the trainer has some knowledge of learning processes and basic memory functions. For those who need more expertise in memory functions and impairments, reading Dehn (2010) or some comparable text (e.g., Emilien, Durlach, Antoniadis, Van Der Linden, & Maloteaux, 2004; Tulving & Craik, 2000) is recommended.

Research Base

All of the methods promoted in this workbook are evidence-based. References and research summaries for nearly all of the methods can be found in one of the Dehn texts

(2008, 2010). Some of the methods have been adapted from the typical format, and some methods have been combined. These adjustments are based on the author's experiences working with students who have memory impairments. You may also recognize some methods from study skills curricula. The objective of most study skills is to commit academic material to memory. Many study skills work because they apply evidence-based memory strategies. You also may discover that some traditional memory methods, such as acronyms, are not included in this workbook. The main reason for such omissions is that these methods are not supported in contemporary memory research. Other memory techniques often found in memory self-help books are not included because they are more for adult everyday functioning, such as the method used to remember names.

General Directions and Principles

For the training program to be successful, you should adhere to the directions and principles described below.

1. Conduct training during brief (maximum of 50 minutes), focused sessions held at least two times per week over a period of at least eight weeks.

2. If the program is being conducted with a group instead of an individual, it will be necessary to differentiate instruction so that the needs of each individual are addressed. For example, some individuals will need more practice, and some will need to practice at different levels of difficulty.

3. Discuss, explain, elaborate, and repeat as much as necessary for the student to understand the concepts and procedures. Pay special attention to any aspects of the method that generally are difficult to understand. Limit your explanations to the topic and concepts presented in each lesson.

4. For lower level students, have the student read the material aloud. If the student is unable to read the material fluently, read it for him or her. If the student has difficulty writing responses, accept his or her oral responses and record them in the workbook.

5. When lessons are short, more than one may be covered in a session. When lessons are challenging, they may require more than one session. Regardless of how many methods are covered in one session, be sure to allow enough time to fully complete any practice exercise that is begun.

6. For each exercise designed to strengthen working memory, regular, ongoing, and challenging practice is necessary. During ongoing working memory exercises, adapt materials downward or upward as needed. For the practice to be effective, it needs to be sufficiently challenging. The student's memory functions are unlikely to improve if the practice is too easy or too difficult.

7. For each memory strategy, provide multiple practice sessions that permit the strategy to be learned to the point where it becomes automatic, or at least applied independently. Also, during practice sessions, provide feedback on how correctly the procedures are being followed. See Appendix A for the minimum number of practice rounds that are recommended.

8. Sometimes it may be difficult for the student to keep directions and steps in mind while trying to practice or apply a new strategy. That is, learning the strategy and trying to remember the material overloads the student's working memory. When this happens, break the procedures into smaller steps and provide as much support as necessary.

9. The student is expected to perform poorly when he or she attempts to memorize workbook materials using his or her usual method or no method at all. His or her failure will help to illustrate how much more effective a new memory strategy can be.

10. At the beginning of each session, do some review of concepts and methods introduced and practiced during previous sessions. The review and redundancy built into the program are intentional, as they support memory. Do not omit content simply because it was covered earlier.

11. For upper level students in particular, inform the student about the purpose and rationale for the strategy, including when, where, and why to use the strategy. Also, explain the benefits and how its use will result in better memory performance. Without this metamemory knowledge, it is less likely that the student will generalize and maintain the newly learned strategy.

12. When introducing a complex strategy, model all the steps and components while thinking aloud. Be sure to bring your modeling down to the student's level and be more of a "coping" or "struggling" model than one whose performance is immediately perfect. Use different examples when modeling, and demonstrate increased understanding and proficiency as you continue modeling.

13. Provide plenty of relevant practice, first with external guidance, then with the student thinking aloud, and finally while encouraging the student to internalize the strategy, such as having the student whisper the steps while enacting them.

14. Give the student positive reinforcement for using new strategies outside of the training sessions.

15. Frequently show the student his or her memory recall data so that the student understands the personal effectiveness of strategy use (see the "Data Collection" section below and Data Collection forms in Appendix B).

16. Encourage the student to monitor and evaluate strategy use and to attribute his or her success to strategy use.

17. Encourage generalization by discussing applications of the strategy and practicing the strategy with different materials and under different situations.

18. Incorporate material the student needs to study or memorize for class into the training as much as possible (see the "Additional Materials" section).

19. Take notes during and after the sessions. Information to record includes student reactions, student performance, and reminders for future sessions. For example, you might note what needs additional practice in upcoming sessions.

Exercises Versus Strategies

Exercises are defined as methods designed to generally improve brain–based memory capacity, functioning, or performance. These exercises are not explicitly strategies that can be generalized or applied to learning (although the student may acquire a basic strategy while practicing them). Also, the exercises are mainly designed to enhance short-term and working memory, not long-term memory. In contrast, *strategies* are memory methods (often referred to as *mnemonics*) designed to improve learning and various aspects of memory (Worthen & Hunt, 2011). These strategies are not intended to remediate or increase memory functions and capacity, but rather to allow the student to more effectively utilize the memory abilities he or she possesses.

Metamemory

If you want the trainee to generalize and maintain the skills learned in this program, the teaching and persistent reinforcement of metamemory is crucial. Essentially, metamemory consists of understanding how memory works; understanding one's memory strengths and weaknesses; understanding how and why memory strategies work; and controlling, regulating, and influencing one's memory processes (Schneider, 2010). Reinforcement of metamemory is embedded throughout the program; for example, showing the trainee how his or her retention improves from using a new method supports metamemory. In the upper level workbook, metamemory factors are directly discussed. Thus, it is very important to retain the metamemory lessons, especially those at the beginning of the workbook, even though they are not explicitly teaching new memory strategies.

Data Collection

Collecting and maintaining data will enable you to monitor and document the student's progress. In Appendix B, you will find forms for keeping track of the student's performance during exercises and strategy practice rounds. It's also important to collect the student's scores from classroom tests, especially those for which the student has switched to new memorization methods. The "Review" and "Reflection" sections allow some formative evaluation as the training progresses. For upper level students, the last three lessons include summative data collection and evaluation of the training.

Additional Materials

Some additional materials for practice, such as vocabulary lists and science, social studies, and literature lessons, can be found in Appendix F. You, the trainer, will need to provide the following additional materials: a stopwatch, index cards, lined paper, arithmetic flash cards, and a deck of regular playing cards. If this training program is conducted during the summer, you will also need to provide ability-appropriate literature, a science text, and a social studies text. For younger children, an ability-appropriate spelling book is recommended. During the school year, you should incorporate the student's scholastic materials and texts as much as possible. For example, spelling books can be used at the lower level, foreign language texts at the upper level, and science and social studies texts at any grade. Just prior to classroom tests are opportune times to incorporate these materials.

CD-ROM

Extra copies of student workbook pages may be printed from the CD-ROM that comes with this workbook. It may be convenient to have the student write on pages printed from the CD-ROM so that you can have the workbook directions in front of you. The CD-ROM also contains data collection forms, as well as grids for playing a visual-spatial game.

Internet Resources

Additional word lists for practicing various memorization strategies are not provided because they can easily be obtained on the Internet by using word list generators. For example, the Paivio et al. Word List Generator containing 925 nouns can be found at www.math.yorku.ca/SCS/Online/paivio. In using this word list generator, you can select how many words you want in the list, how many letters and syllables they should contain, and how concrete, imaginable, and meaningful the words are. With younger children, you should typically use one- and two-syllable words; with older children, you should typically use two- and three-syllable words. When practicing visualization of words, you should select words that are rated high on concreteness and imagery. As the student improves in performance, you can select more challenging words. Another Internet word list generator, which has a database of 2,084 words, can be found at www .wordlistgenerator.net.

In addition to the working memory exercises found in the workbook, evidence-based, game-like working memory training programs can be found on the Internet. One example is Jungle Memory, found at www.junglememory.com. Another is CogMed, found at www.cogmed.com. There is a fee for both programs. Neither is connected with this workbook or the workbook's author.

Communication With Teachers and Parents

Regardless of the setting in which the training is conducted, it is important to involve and communicate with teachers and parents throughout the course of training. Not only does this encourage teachers and parents to prompt and reinforce the student's application of new memory strategies, it also helps the student, especially if he or she is a younger student, understand the importance and relevance of the training. Also, parents can provide additional practice time with the exercises designed to strengthen working memory performance. An effective method of communication is a note after each lesson that explains what was practiced and that provides suggestions for how the student should be applying the new strategies. For concerned and involved teachers and parents, it is helpful to allow these teachers and parents to observe at least some of the sessions. The author of this workbook has discovered that student trainees are even more successful when their teachers or parents regularly observe the training sessions. These informed teachers and parents can then provide additional practice and encourage ongoing use of the new memory strategies.

Optional Pre- and Post-Tests

If there has not been any formal memory testing, it would be helpful to conduct a basic, informal test of the student's auditory (verbal) short-term memory span and of the student's delayed recall of verbal material before beginning any training. This pre-intervention data can help determine starting levels for working memory exercises and set realistic expectations for the student's performance with strategy practice materials. When the training is complete, a post-test may be administered. The post-intervention data can be compared with the initial results to see if there has been an increase in immediate or delayed retention. However, the difference between pre- and post-test scores should not be used to evaluate the overall success of the memory training. Real world changes in memory performance, such as improved scores on classroom exams, will provide a more valid assessment of progress.

The pre- and post-tests are in Appendix K and on the CD-ROM. You should print out the test you are using so that you can score responses on that sheet.

Lesson-by-Lesson Directions

Grade Level Recommendations

The lower level workbook is intended for students in grades 3 through 6 who have average intellectual abilities. The lower level workbook is also appropriate for older students with below average abilities, learning disabilities, or significant memory impairments. Students in grades 1 and 2 may be able to benefit from the more basic strategies, namely rehearsal methods (Lessons 11–16), dual encoding (Lessons 22–23), and visualization strategies (Lessons 22 and 25). The upper level workbook is intended for students in grades 7 through 12 and college students who have learning and memory challenges. Some of the lessons found only in the upper level book may be appropriate for some sixth graders. If the materials for practicing memorization are too easy or too difficult, the corresponding materials for the other age level may be used.

Arrangement of the Workbook Lessons

The memory lessons are categorized and briefly described below.

Lessons 1 to 8

At both levels, these cover basic memory structures and processes, the individual's memory strengths and weaknesses, an assessment of and introduction to metamemory, an assessment of strategy use, and goal setting.

Lesson 9

The purpose of this crucial lesson is to demonstrate to the student the potential efficacy of memory strategies. The task varies by age level.

Lesson 10

At both levels, this is the first of several opportunities for review and reflection.

Lessons 11 to 18

At both levels, these lessons cover a variety of rehearsal strategies and their applications to academics.

Lessons 19 to 21

At both levels, these are exercises, not strategies, designed to improve short-term and working memory performance and possibly increase memory span.

Lessons 22 to 28

At both levels, these lessons consist of mnemonics designed to improve long-term memory encoding, consolidation, retention, and retrieval.

Lessons 29 to 36

At both levels, these lessons involve more in-depth processing of information and strategies that are closely related with academic study skills.

Lessons 37 to 39

At both levels, these lessons include strategies and materials for coping with everyday memory problems. They are intended more for students with severe memory impairments.

Lesson 40 (Lower Level Only)

This final lesson for the lower level addresses the student's plans for continued strategy use.

Lesson 40 (Upper Level Only)

This lesson trains the keyword mnemonic, a strategy that would be fairly difficult for younger students.

Lessons 41 to 47

These upper level lessons consist primarily of advanced study skills designed to enhance long-term retention of information.

Lessons 48 to 50

These upper level lessons are evaluation and planning materials.

How Lesson Directions Are Organized

The first section under each lesson applies to both the lower and upper level workbooks. If necessary, this section is followed by directions specific to each level. Anything that you need to orally present to the student is printed in **bold**. You should read the "General Directions and Principles" section before attempting any lessons. Just prior to each lesson, read the material on the student's workbook pages. Also, be sure to completely read the trainer's directions for a lesson before beginning that lesson. It is important to adhere to the guidelines. If they are ignored or loosely applied, the effectiveness of the lessons will be diminished. As a result, the student may not learn, maintain, or generalize the strategies very well, or benefit from the memory exercises.

Lesson 1: Introduction for Students

The main purpose of this lesson is to introduce students to the workbook and the memory training they are about to receive. Another important purpose is to help them recognize that they are not alone; everyone has problems remembering information. Finally, this lesson lays the groundwork for an initial discussion of their feelings about memory.

At the end of the first paragraph, ask the student if he or she agrees that everyone forgets things at least some of the time. Then ask the student for examples of things that he or she forgets. If the student is hesitant, talk briefly about the kinds of things you forget. Then look at the graphs and reinforce how quickly people forget new information. Also point out that how quickly we learn something does not determine how well we will remember it later. Some students take longer to learn something, but then remember it well for a long period of time. Others, who quickly learn new material, may also quickly forget it.

After reading the second paragraph, you might have a discussion with the student about why he or she needs memory training, especially if no one has previously discussed the need for training with the student. You might also indicate that during a later lesson, the student will have a chance to set some goals for memory improvement.

After reading the third paragraph, look at and discuss the illustration of the brain's memory center and storage areas. Then, briefly answer any questions the student might have, but do not discuss specifics of memory functioning or the student's memory strengths and weaknesses at this time.

Lower Level Directions

With young children, one option is to allow the child to color in the different brain lobes as you discuss their functions. Another option is to have the student point to different parts of his or her head to show you he or she understands where the different lobes are located. It might also be helpful to explain that the frontal lobe, the part responsible for using special memory methods, is still developing. The implication is that the child is not expected to know or have developed all of the memory methods that will be taught in this workbook.

Upper Level Directions

The text in the upper level is more adult-like than the lower level. If the text is too challenging, you might switch to the lower level to make it more understandable. With older, high ability students, it may be helpful to impress upon them the fact that there is a neurological basis to memory. That is, memory is not just a matter of effort, desire, and will. If a student was born with a weaker memory center or has acquired a memory problem, he or she will need to learn the strategies in this workbook to compensate for that biological weakness.

Lesson 2: Thoughts and Feelings About Memory

The purpose of this lesson is threefold: first, to assess the student's understanding of his or her memory strengths and weaknesses; second, to determine how well the student understands memory functions and memory systems; and third, to gain some insight into how the student feels about his or her memory performance.

There is a counseling aspect to effective memory training that initially comes into play as you and the student process the answers to the lesson's questions. The student's answers will allow you to explore and understand how much self-awareness (metamemory) and acceptance the student has regarding his or her memory problems. Also, the feelings, such as frustration, associated with memory failures also need to be acknowledged before memory strategies are taught. The possibility of denial on the part of the student may also become evident at this point, but do not confront the student at this stage. Accept his or her answers for now.

Encourage the student to answer each question; don't accept "don't know" as a response. To encourage a response, you might share what you would provide for an answer. It is important to have the student write in the responses or that you record them so that there is record of the student's knowledge of memory at the beginning of the training. If necessary, explain the basic difference between short-term and long-term memory when the student comes to questions 6 and 7. After all the responses have been written in, go back and discuss any that you believe need elaboration or clarification. If the student has many questions about memory, delay answering questions that will be addressed in later lessons.

Lesson 3: How Memory Works

The more a child or adolescent understands about how memory works, the more he or she will be able to effectively utilize the training in this book. At a minimum, the student needs to recognize the basic differences between short-term and long-term memory (Baddeley, Eysenck, & Anderson, 2009). The student also needs to know that each memory system is divided into auditory and visual, and that long-term memories for personal experiences are different from long-term memories for facts and knowledge.

After the student looks at the illustration of the movement of information through different kinds of memory, check for understanding by having the student explain the flow of information and by having the student identify the different types of memory. Provide explanations and examples as needed.

Do not provide help when the student completes the memory quiz, except to write the responses for the student if necessary. The quiz is intended to function as a review, as well as to allow you to assess how well the student is grasping the material. Review any items the student misses or does not seem to understand.

Lower Level Directions

At the end of the first paragraph, orally present these five words at the rate of one per second:

Biscuit   Elbow   Raccoon   Video   Window

Have the student recall them as soon as you finish presenting them. Then have the student recall them again after he or she finishes reading the paragraph on long-term memory. There is no need to record or tally the student's responses.

At this age level, the concept of working memory has been omitted in order to keep things simple. For older, more capable students who need to understand their specific working memory weakness, go to the upper level and read and explain the paragraph on working memory. Then show them the upper level figure on the flow of information. For those who don't need to know about working memory, you should attribute working memory functions to short-term memory (Oakes & Bauer, 2007).

If you think the student does not understand why he or she needs help with memory, it might be helpful to read the story about Kim found at the end of the upper level lesson.

Upper Level Directions

At the end of the first paragraph, orally present these eight words at the rate of one per second:

Biscuit   Garage   Elbow   Internet   Raccoon   Video   Melon   Window

Have the student recall them as soon as you finish presenting them. Then have the student recall them again after he or she finishes reading the paragraph on long-term memory. There is no need to record or tally the student's responses.

At the end of the working memory paragraph, read the student a math problem that must be attempted without pencil or paper. If requested, you may repeat the problem once.

For middle school students, read this problem:

Betty went to the store to buy school supplies. She purchased 15 folders at 10 cents each and 7 pencils at 5 cents each. After she gave the clerk 2 dollars, how much change did she get back?

For high school students, read this problem.

Sam works at an electronics store where he gets a 20 percent discount on anything he buys. He also is allowed to pay for it in 10 interest-free payments. If Sam purchases an item worth $400.00, how much will each of his 10 payments be after he receives his discount?

If the Internet is available, you might play a video of a chimpanzee outperforming college students on a test of short-term and working memory. The video, called "ABC News, Chimps vs. Humans" can be found on YouTube at www.youtube.com/watch?v=cPiDHXtM0VA. The video illustrates that humans have limitations in short-term and working memory.

Discuss the concepts introduced in the paragraph on long-term memory. It is important for older students to understand that there are two long-term memory systems: personal and factual (Schacter, 1996). Also, be sure that the student recognizes that factual memories are not automatically and easily acquired like the personal ones.

Lesson 4: Memory Strengths and Weaknesses

As the student views the illustration at the end of the lesson, first ask the student which parts he or she thinks are the personal strengths and weaknesses. Then, based on any formal or informal assessment data you have, suggest corrections to any student misconceptions. Also, give your impression for any parts the student does not know about. Then, have the student color in all of the components, with different colors for strengths and weaknesses.

Lower Level Directions

For questions 1 and 2, first elicit responses from the student orally. If the student's responses are minimal, suggest other strengths and weaknesses that you know the student possesses.

Upper Level Directions

For items 6 and 7, if the student's responses are minimal, suggest other strengths and weaknesses that you know the student possesses. If you have formal assessment data on the student's memory, this would be an appropriate time to explain the assessment results in child-friendly language, if the child has not heard the results before. When doing so, translate the assessment results in a manner that matches them up with the memory components in the figure at the end of the lesson.

Lesson 5: Memory Beliefs

The purpose of this lesson is to further assess the student's metamemory development by identifying any naïve conceptions the student still holds about memory functioning. All of the items on this page are myths. As children mature, they believe in fewer and fewer memory myths. After the child or adolescent has finished reading and checking the items, inform him or her that none of the items are true. For each item the child has checked, provide a simple explanation.

Lesson 6: Memorization Methods

The purpose of this lesson is to determine which, if any, memorization methods and strategies the student currently employs. Be prepared to provide the student with paper or index cards if requested. Once the student has demonstrated his or her memorization method, there is no need for the student to continue memorizing the words. When the demonstration is complete, have the student explain what he or she was doing and write in the description. With the science lesson, the goal is similar. This time, however, observe how the student might identify and organize the facts, as well as try to rehearse them. Some students will not be able to demonstrate any strategy other than reading the paragraph. The questions on the second page of Lesson 6 allow you to further discuss and assess the student's level of metamemory and memory strategy development.

Lesson 7: Memory Strategies Survey

This lesson is the final assessment piece before training in memory methods and strategies begins. Again, the primary goal is to determine which basic strategies the student might be using on a regular basis. The secondary goal is to keep the student thinking about memory strategy options and to reinforce the idea that there are memory methods that might make a difference. You should discuss any items of which the student seems unsure. Even if the student claims to always use a particular strategy, you should still introduce and train that strategy if it is covered in this workbook. The strategies in the survey are rudimentary strategies and include some "everyday" memory techniques. The list does not include the higher level academic learning strategies that are included in this training program. If the student's response to the last item indicates the use of any other strategies, identify it in writing at the bottom of the page.

Lesson 8: Goals for Improving Memory

Guide the student through the process of writing feasible, specific, and measurable goals that address his or her memory weaknesses. Provide as much discussion and assistance as necessary if the student has difficulty writing goals or writing responses to the first three items on the page. Goals that identify specific performance are more useful than general statements, such as, "I will improve my long-term memory." A more specific and measurable goal might be something like, "I will remember more information that I study for tests." It's all right to have more than three goals. Before accepting any goal, review this workbook to be sure that the memory training will address it. At least two of the goals should pertain to academic learning. Only one should involve everyday memory challenges in the home environment. Try to review the goals with the student on a regular basis, informally assessing progress when you do.

Upper Level Directions

Goal setting at the upper level should involve an in-depth discussion. After the student writes his or her goals, have the student explain why each is important. Next, ask the student how he or she will know when each of the goals has been achieved. For example, an appropriate response would be that improved test scores in a class would indicate goal attainment. The intent of this step is to help the student make the goal concrete and somewhat measureable. Finally, have the student specify a date by which the goal should be achieved. After these steps have been completed, you and the student may decide to revise one or more of the goals. After the student's goal setting is complete, inform the student of the goals that you have for him or her, and then ask the student if he or she agrees with these additional goals.

Lesson 9: A Memory Experiment

Be sure to allow enough time to complete both Parts I and II during the same training session. Also, you will need a stopwatch and an index card or sheet of paper to cover up stimulus words.

The purpose of the memory experiment is to demonstrate to the student that there are memory techniques that make a significant difference in how much is remembered. When the student realizes how much performance can be improved by applying a basic strategy, the student is more likely to "buy into" memory training. Ninety-five percent of the time the results will favor the method in Part II of the experiment. If they do not, proceed with the training course and be sure to emphasize improved performance from strategy use when you first encounter it.

The strategies in this lesson are designed to enhance long-term memory performance, not short-term memory. So, do not allow the student to immediately respond to either set of items. Reading through the "Things That Can Harm Memory" and the "Things That Can Help Memory" sections will create enough of a delay and also prevent the student from further rehearsing the material. Limit the time spent on "Things That Can Harm Memory" to five minutes, and do the same for "Things That Can Help Memory" so that the delay intervals are equivalent.

After recall for both parts of the experiment is complete, tally the number correct. If the student scores higher on Part II, emphasize how using the strategy of visualization or grouping can increase the amount of information we retain in long-term memory. Also, talk about how this means that we do have some control over our memory, and that we can learn to do things that improve performance. If you are regularly consulting with a teacher or parent as you proceed with the training, share the student's improved performance from using the visualization or grouping strategy so that teachers and parents can further reinforce the benefits of memory training.

At the end of the session, be sure to remind the student about the assignment described at the end of the "Part II" section.

Lower Level Directions

Keep the Part I word list covered until the student has read and understood the directions. The student should read the Part I list aloud four times. If the student struggles to pronounce a word or reads it incorrectly, immediately say the word. If the student lacks reading ability, read the Part I list aloud four times. Be sure to cover the words with an index card or something similar after the list has been read four times.

You must read the Part II word list for all students. After saying each item, pause to allow the student to form an image and wait until the student says he or she sees the item before reading the next one.

Part II Word List

Ball	Hammer	Car	Apple	Hat	Lion
Carrot	Mouse	Tree	Church	Phone	Book

Upper Level Directions

Keep the word list covered until the student has read and understood the directions. Then tell the student to point to any unknown words as he or she comes to them. If this happens, immediately say the word. If you suspect the student will have difficulty recognizing several of the words, use the word list from the lower level lesson instead. The student is not required to read the words aloud. Be sure to cover the words with an index card or something similar after one minute has expired.

Keep the word list on the second page covered until the student has read and understood the directions. Again, cover the words with an index card or something similar after one minute has expired.

Lesson 10: Review and Reflections

This is the first of several opportunities for reflection and review. The student's responses will provide some feedback about what the student is learning and how he or she is feeling about the training. After the written responses are complete, discuss with the student his or her thoughts and feelings.

Lesson 11: Repetition

Beginning with Lesson 11, reviews of previous lessons and recall of memorized material will frequently be inserted at the beginning of lessons. You should also review, discuss, and practice any other strategies that you think the student has not yet fully grasped or mastered (see the practice recommendations in Appendix A).

The purpose of this lesson is to teach the student to use cumulative repetition. Developmentally, repetition, or rehearsal, is one of the first memory strategies an individual acquires. Repetition allows a person to maintain information in short-term memory for longer intervals. Longer maintenance of information in short-term memory increases the odds that the information will get encoded into long-term memory. However, simple rehearsal is a relatively weak strategy for ensuring long-term retention.

Lower Level Directions

For Practice Round 1, say the following words at the rate of two seconds per word:

Knee   Work   Gun   Fall   Horn   Fire   Race

When you have finished reading the list, have the student immediately recall the words. Tally the number correct and record it in the student's workbook.

For Practice Round 2, make sure the student understands the procedure by practicing with these three words: **dog, cat, bee**. The student should keep saying "dog" until you say "cat," and then should repeat "dog, cat" until you say "bee," after which the student should keep repeating "dog, cat, bee." Then, present the seven words listed below. Before presenting the next word, allow the student to repeat (or try to repeat) the sequence twice. Do not allow rehearsal after you present the last word. Instead, immediately say, "Tell me all the words."

Beans   Lemon   Fish   Milk   Salt   Bread   Coffee

Tally the number correct and record it in the student's workbook. If the student performs better on Practice Round 2, explain that the increased performance is due to the cumulative rehearsal method used in Round 2.

Upper Level Directions

For Practice Round 2, make sure the student understands the procedure by practicing with these three words: **pancake, muscle, curtain**. The student should keep saying "pancake" until you say "muscle," and then should repeat "pancake, muscle" until you say "curtain," after which the student should keep repeating all three words in sequence. Then, present the 10 words listed below. Before presenting the next word, allow the student to repeat the sequence once. When finished, have the student immediately and orally recall the words as you mark the correct responses.

Winter	Barrel	Tiger	Dream	Wheat
Hotel	Creek	Office	Tunnel	Father

Lesson 12: Repeating Written Information

During Practice Round 1 have the student whisper the words loud enough so that you can hear them. Also, have the student go through the list at least five times, but no more than 10. Use an index card to cover the words while the student writes them in the right-hand column.

For Practice Round 2, provide paper for the student to copy each word five times. When finished, the student should write the recalled words in the workbook. If the student performs better with one method than the other, discuss the possibility that the student's memory works better when that approach is used. The final question in the lesson is to prompt the student to think about the possibility of combining two memorization methods. To help the student remember the assignment and spelling book for next time, you might write the information in the student's daily assignment notebook if available.

Lesson 13: Using Repetition to Study Spelling

Be prepared to provide grade-appropriate spelling words if the student does not bring his or her spelling book. Be sure the student completes each step of the procedure exactly as directed. Discuss with the student that this procedure increases memorability because the correct spelling goes into more than one kind of memory. Use this method to help the student study for an upcoming spelling test. If the student's spelling test scores improve after this lesson or Lesson 16, attribute the improvement to the use of these new memorization strategies. Encourage the student to continue using these methods to study spelling.

Lesson 14: Chunking

In addition to rehearsal, chunking is a basic strategy that improves short-term memory performance. If the student has difficulty keeping his or her place in the numbers while chunking, have the student draw lines between the chunks before saying them. If additional practice with chunking is planned, record how many digits the student remembers when chunking.

Lesson 15: Review of Repetition and Chunking

Accept oral responses to review items 1–3; there's no need for the student to write the responses. Make sure the student understands that he or she should use cumulative rehearsal (adding one word at time) when listening, but just go through the entire list several times when reading. For the basic repetition practice, have the student do it without chunking. For the second set of practice items, the student should keep the words in groups of three while rehearsing them several times. Compare the student's recall for both lists. If the student does better with the combined method, point out that combining two methods often produces better results.

Lesson 16: Using Chunking to Memorize Spelling

If the student has a difficult time recognizing syllables, have the student place a hand under his or her jaw while saying the words aloud. The student will be able to feel his or her jaw drop at the beginning of each syllable. If necessary, help the student draw lines segmenting the words into syllables before allowing the oral rehearsal. Also, make the student pause briefly after saying the letters in each chunk.

The student's responses to the "Thoughts About Memory Training" section will provide you with feedback about how the student views the potential benefits of rehearsal and chunking. If the student is able to write responses, have him or her do so without prompting to prevent biasing the responses. After the writing is complete, discuss the student's thoughts and feelings. At the end of this lesson, ask the student to bring a science or social studies book to the next session.

Upper Level Directions

If you decide to do this lesson but did not have the student complete Lessons 12, 13, and 15, then there is no need to complete the Thoughts About Memory Training questions.

Lesson 17: Putting Words Into Sentences and Stories

For the sentences part of this lesson, have the student tell you each sentence before writing it. The sentences should be focused and make sense. Funny sentences are ideal, but not necessary. It's also better if the sentence describes some action, rather than just states a fact. During the recall phase, have the student say the sentence first, and then write down the stimulus word.

For the story exercise, have the student discuss the idea of the story before trying to write it. To keep it focused, require the student to have at least one stimulus word in each sentence. Do not allow the student to simply list several of the stimulus words in one sentence. During recall, the student should retell the story instead of just writing down the words without recalling the story.

During this lesson or a subsequent lesson, help the student apply one of these approaches to words or facts that need to be memorized for science or social studies. When applying these methods to coursework, facts can be used instead of just isolated words. For example, the fact that George Washington was the first president of the United States can be woven into a story. When trying to apply this approach, do not allow the student to just retell what is presented in the textbook. The student should create his or her own story that incorporates the facts.

Upper Level Directions

To demonstrate the potential effectiveness of the story method for academic material, you might complete the assignment with the student. First, have the student study a science or social studies chapter subsection as he or she normally would. Then, have the student study a comparable subsection by incorporating key words and facts into a story. After both methods are completed, you should make up five to ten questions for each subsection. You can use these questions at the beginning of the next session to check recall and compare methods.

Lesson 18: Comparing Memory Methods

This lesson initiates the testing of retention for material studied during previous lessons. In most cases, the student will remember more information when he or she uses a strategy, or uses a more elaborate strategy. When this happens, take advantage of the teachable moment to reinforce the idea that a memory strategy is better than no strategy at all, and also that some strategies are more effective than others. With this lesson for instance, the child will probably recall fewer words memorized with the repetition and chunking method than with the other methods. If so, point out that repetition and chunking primarily benefit short-term retention, not long-term retention, and that is why the student needs to learn more involved methods.

Upper Level Directions

Older students should have previously studied two subsections from one of their textbooks, putting key words and facts into a story for the second subsection. Now quiz them about each section, using questions that you created. It is okay if this is done somewhat informally. If the student performs noticeably better on the second subsection, discuss this with the student and attribute it to using a more elaborate memory strategy than simple repetition.

Lesson 19: Using Arithmetic to Build Memory

This lesson initiates exercises designed to increase the capacity of working memory. In order for working memory to improve, the exercises must be challenging and done on a regular basis (Doidge, 2007; Klingberg, 2009). Once the student masters one level, keep it challenging by adding another item to remember. For example, once the student can remember the sequence of answers for three arithmetic problems, require him or her to remember four answers in a row. The student should be able to recall the answer sequences correctly for 10 consecutive sets of problems before another arithmetic problem is added. During this lesson, keep increasing the span until the student is not able to do 10 sequences successfully. This level then becomes the baseline. Continue from this level when the student does this exercise during subsequent training sessions. See Appendix A for a recommended practice schedule.

The arithmetic flash cards used (you will need to provide these) should be grade-appropriate, but also at the child's skill level. That is, the arithmetic calculations should be relatively easy. Do not use this method if the child lacks arithmetic fluency with even basic addition, such as children who must finger count to compute the answer. Instead, use the card exercise introduced in Lesson 20. One of these exercises should be used for a few minutes during each lesson. (Parents might also be encouraged to do one of them with the child at home.) You may keep track of the student's progress on one of the data collection sheets found in Appendix B.

Parents should be asked to play this memory game with the child or adolescent at home. If you suggest this to a parent, send home the instruction sheet found in Appendix M.

Upper Level Directions

After the student reads the section on working memory overload in the classroom, have a discussion with the student about the signs of overload and how this affects academic performance. Reinforce the idea that this happens to everyone; it's just a matter of how often it happens. The implication of this section is that completing challenging working memory exercises (this one or the ones in Lessons 20 and 21) designed to strengthen working memory will pay off when the student is able to handle more information in the classroom without getting overloaded.

Lesson 20: Using Cards to Build Memory

The n-back activity is another evidence-based exercise designed to promote working memory growth. A regular deck of playing cards can be used. For younger children who struggle with 2-back, remove the face cards from the deck. N-back involves remembering a number or some other item a certain number of items ago. Here is an example of 2-back, using a deck of playing cards: if the cards displayed and removed one at time are 6—9—4—5, the student should say "six" when the 4 is displayed, "nine" when the 5 is displayed, and so on.

After the child understands the task, mix up the deck of cards and show each card one at time. After displaying the card for about two seconds, remove it from the student's view, but keep it in your view so that you know the sequence when the student responds. The student must name the n-back card as soon as another card is flipped over. When the student makes the first error, stop, reshuffle the cards, and begin again. When the student successfully answers 10 in a row three times, require the student to remember another card back. For example, when going to from 2-back to 3-back with 6—9—4—5, the student must wait until the 5 is displayed before saying "six."

When introducing this game, begin with 1-back and continue to increase the number back until the student is no longer able to respond correctly 10 times in a row. This level then becomes the baseline. Continue from this level when the student does this exercise during subsequent training sessions. Use the data sheet in Appendix B to keep track of progress.

After a certain point, the student will not be able to advance without some sort of strategy. If the student reports no strategy use, suggest that he or she use silent repetition while dropping and adding a number or face card each time. For example, using the 6—9—4—5 sequence with 2-back, tell the child to keeping saying "six, nine" until the four is flipped up, then say "six" and then keep repeating "nine, four" until the next card is flipped up, and so on. This strategy is explained in writing in the Upper Level workbook but not the Lower Level.

Parents should be asked to play this memory game with the child or adolescent at home. If you try this option, send home the *n*-back instruction sheet found in Appendix M.

Lower Level Directions

During this lesson read the story of Jesse to the student. The story about Jesse can be used as a starter for a discussion on how the student is currently feeling about his or her memory problems, as well as how he or she is feeling about the memory training and specific strategies. You might begin by asking the student if he or she knows anyone like Jesse, and then proceed by asking if the student has ever had the same feelings as Jesse.

Lesson 21: Remembering Locations to Build Memory

This exercise is designed to increase visual-spatial short-term memory. Ongoing practice at a sufficient level of difficulty is recommended (see Appendix A). The items on the lesson page should allow you to determine at approximately what level practice should continue. To complete the items on the page, cover up all but one at a time. Display an item for five seconds, and then have the student immediately reproduce what he or she recalls on the blank grid to the right. Then go on to the next item. In order to count as correct, both the shape and the location need to be correct.

When conducting this exercise you can save paper by using a "game board" approach. From Appendix I on the CD-ROM, print the grid size that you need. The available grids are 2×2, 3×3, 4×4, and 5×5. Then, using chips of two different colors, such as red and black chips, randomly place the appropriate number of chips in game board cells. Arrange the chips out of the student's sight, and record the arrangement if it is difficult for you to remember. Display the arrangement for five seconds and then remove the chips. Do not hand these chips to the student. Rather, the student should then use his or her own pile of chips to make the placement he or she recalls. Record whether the student's response is correct and then arrange and present another item. Follow the same procedure used with the exercises in the two previous lessons. Once the student can successfully complete 10 items in a row at a particular level, advance to the next level. You may keep track of the student's progress on the data collection sheet found in Appendix B.

Here are the levels of difficulty in ascending order:

2×2 grid
 1 red chip
 1 red chip and 1 black chip

3×3 grid
 1 red chip and 1 black chip
 2 red chips and 1 black chip
 2 red chips and 2 black chips

4×4 grid
 2 red chips and 2 black chips
 3 red chips and 2 black chips
 3 red chips and 3 black chips

5×5 grid
 3 red chips and 3 black chips
 4 red chips and 3 black chips
 4 red chips and 4 black chips

Lesson 22: Picturing Verbal Information

For lower level students, this lesson is similar to Lesson 9. However, do not skip this lesson, because learning to consciously visualize verbal information is a crucial encoding skill. For Practice Round 1, read the words if the student lacks reading fluency. Pause for a couple seconds between each word. Read through the list as many times as you can in one minute. Cover the words when you or the student has finished reading them.

After the student reads and checks items under the "Helping Your Memory in the Classroom" section, take a few minutes to discuss the importance of each suggestion (Gathercole & Alloway, 2008). Then help the student select a new behavior that he or she is willing to try in the coming weeks. During later sessions, inquire as to whether the student has adopted this behavior and whether he or she thinks it might be supporting his or her short-term or working memory.

Make sure the student understands the task before beginning Practice Round 2. Also, inform the student that he or she should take some time with each word, because there is no time limit for this round, and that he or she should only go through the list once. If it's necessary to read the items to the student, pause for five seconds between each word.

Do the same for the "Helping Your Memory at Home" section as you did for the "Helping Your Memory in the Classroom" section.

For the "Visualizing Directions" section, see the level-specific material below. When finished reading the directions to the student, immediately have the student describe the images he or she created for each step. If the student did not place himself or herself in the scenes, direct him or her to do so while you read the directions again. Then ask the student to verbally recall the directions in order.

Lower Level Directions

For the "Visualizing Directions" section, read these step-by-step directions slowly:

Imagine you are in the classroom and your teacher gives you these personal directions to follow:

1. **First, pick up the brown envelope from my desk and take it with you.**
2. **Next, go to the classroom across the hallway and ask the teacher for the package she would like mailed.**
3. **Next, take both the envelope and the package down to the principal's secretary.**
4. **Then, ask the secretary for the birthday cake that has been delivered and bring it back with you.**
5. **On the way past the lunchroom, ask one of the cooks if you can have some silverware for the cake and bring the silverware back with you.**

Upper Level Directions

For the "Visualizing Directions" section, read the first five steps under the Lower Level Directions above and then add these three steps:

6. **When you get back to the room, quietly take the cake and put in on my chair behind the desk so that no one will see it.**
7. **And then put the silverware quietly down on my desk.**
8. **Then return to your desk, and finish working on your art project.**

After the student has recalled the directions, remind the student that visualizing works because it creates two different memory codes: verbal and visual. Then, discuss how visualizing can be applied to different kinds of verbal information. Next, have the student suggest some subjects, material, or situations for which he or she thinks the method would be really effective. Finally, help the student develop a plan for trying visualizing during the upcoming weeks.

Lesson 23: Naming and Describing What You See

The purpose of this lesson is to demonstrate how to verbalize visual information. Along with Lesson 22, this lesson reinforces the importance of dual encoding. If the student does not attempt to reproduce a figure, tell the student to draw as much of the figure as he or she can remember.

Lower Level Directions

For Practice Round 1, allow the student only 15 seconds to view the figures, then cover them up and have the student immediately draw them on a separate sheet of paper. For Practice Round 2, have the student describe each figure aloud before going on to the next one. If the second set of figures is reproduced more accurately than the first set, reinforce the value of verbalizing visual information.

Upper Level Directions

Older children (10 years or older) tend to name objects naturally. However, they still need to understand the benefits of verbalizing, and also become aware of how to apply the method broadly. For example, they need to realize that spatial locations are more memorable when they are described. After Practice Round 3, give the student more examples of verbalizing visual information, such as describing pictures and graphics found in textbooks.

Lesson 24: Grouping Words by Category

For upper level students, this lesson is similar to Lesson 9. However, do not skip this lesson, because learning to categorize and organize information is a crucial encoding skill.

Lower Level Directions

For Practice Round 1, read the words if the student lacks reading fluency. Pause for a couple seconds between each word. Read through the list as many times as you can in one minute and then cover up the words.

There is no time limit for Practice Round 2. Provide clues if the student has difficulty recognizing the categories. The categories are furniture, fruit, transportation, and communication. After the student has finished writing, direct the student to first memorize the names of the categories before studying the items in each category. If the student's recall is better for Round 2, stress the benefits of categorization and organization.

Younger students may need assistance with Practice Round 3. The science facts should be grouped under blood, digestion, and excretion. At the end of the lesson, help the student identify academic material for which categorizing and reorganizing information would be appropriate.

Upper Level Directions

After the student finishes reading the first paragraph, tell the student to immediately answer the questions you are about to ask. Then hold up a sheet of white paper and say,

"What color is this paper?" As soon as the student says "white" ask, **"What do cows drink?"** Ninety-five percent of students will say "milk" and then smile or laugh as they realize the answer is probably "water." Explain to the student that this happened because the student was in his or her "white things" memory file and that the closest memory link between "white" and "cow" is "milk." Then give examples of categorical memory files that most people have, such as animals, schools, toys, and so on. Then ask the student to give some other examples of his or her memory files.

For Practice Round 1, provide clues if the student has difficulty recognizing the categories. The categories are mathematics, communication, earth formations, and rulers or elected officials. After the student recalls the words by category, point out that categorization and reorganization of information is an encoding method that will improve the long-term storage and retrieval of that information, not just immediate recall.

For Practice Round 2, provide clues if necessary. The categories are religion, locations in the city, and things they created. Finish the lesson with a discussion about other ways of organizing and reorganizing information and about which class materials categorizing and organizing would be effective for. Ask the student to bring an example of information he or she has categorized or organized to a later session.

Lesson 25: Imagining Yourself in the Scene

When students imagine themselves as observers in scenes from literature or history, the information becomes much more memorable (Grilli & Glisky, 2010), especially when they think about how they were feeling as they imagined being there.

Lower Level Directions

If necessary, read the practice story to the student. After the story has been read, ask the student to describe what he or she saw and felt while he or she was in the scene.

Lesson 26: Using Locations to Remember Information

Loci is the first visual mnemonic introduced in the workbook. Loci works because the items to be remembered are paired with personal things the individual already knows and won't forget. If the student has difficulty coming up with enough large items in his or her bedroom, suggest items such as a window, closet, or pictures on the wall.

As the student describes images of the pairings, or associations, make sure the images meet the following criteria:

1. The objects or rooms are used in sequence; don't allow skipping around.
2. There is some kind of action or interaction in the image; just picturing the two items together is not very memorable.

3. The image should be funny, unusual, or even bizarre.
4. The image should be limited to the object and the item to be associated with it. Introducing irrelevant elements reduces effectiveness.
5. Images created by the student are more memorable than ones that you supply.

For example, if a Siberian tiger is paired with a student's bedroom dresser, an appropriate image might be the tiger digging through the drawers with the clothes flying in all directions. This would be more effective than a tiger simply sitting atop the dresser.

Lower Level Directions

The extent of follow-up practice with this mnemonic depends on the child's age and success with the method. Whether there is additional practice also depends on how well the method applies to academic materials the student currently needs to memorize.

Upper Level Directions

If the student says that there are not eight rooms in his or her home, help break it down so that there are enough. For example, an entryway, stairs, hallway, and a closet could be used.

For higher level students, you might play an Internet video that demonstrates a variation of the loci method. If you do, explain to the student that the demonstration in the video is different because two words are being associated with each location instead of just one word. It's also different because the individual does not go through the home locations in any sequence. Stress the importance of going through the rooms or objects in order so that you will know when a word is missing. The video, called "Andi Bell explains the link method memory technique (2/2)" can be found on YouTube at www .youtube.com/watch?v=9NROegsMqNc.

Lesson 27: Pegword

The pegwords must be learned before this mnemonic can be used successfully. The fact that each pegword rhymes with its associated number makes it more memorable. During practice have the student describe each image to you. Images should be focused and funny. If they are not, help the student revise them. After the practice rounds, have a discussion with the student about other types of information or situations for which using pegwords would be a good strategy.

Lesson 28: Review and Reflections

For students who lack writing fluency, accept oral responses and record their responses in the workbook.

Lesson 29: Using Study Cards

You will need to provide index cards for this lesson. For those students who have regularly been using study cards, there is still a need for additional practice rounds to ensure that they are studying from them correctly (see the rules or tips on the student's page). At the end of the lesson, remind all grade levels to bring a science or social studies text to the next lesson.

Lower Level Directions

As the student practices with the Spanish vocabulary study cards, make sure that he or she is following all the rules. Only terms that the student immediately knows should go into the "know" pile. After all the cards reach the "know" pile, go through the procedures once more before testing recall. At the end of the lesson, encourage the student to make study cards for an academic subject and bring the cards to the next lesson.

Upper Level Directions

After the student finishes creating a set of study cards, have the student explain how he or she currently uses them to study before he or she reads the procedures under "Practice Round 2" and the following section on tips. During Practice Round 2, make sure the student is following the sorting and mixing procedures. After the student reads the tips, check for understanding. Then emphasize that study cards will be significantly more effective and efficient if the procedures and tips in this lesson are adopted. Finally, ask the student to bring some study cards to future lessons so that he or she can demonstrate how to use them effectively.

Lesson 30: Thinking About the Information

Elaboration is effective because it involves in-depth processing of information and because the learner consciously and directly links new information to related prior knowledge. That is, associations are made between new facts and existing facts during encoding. These linkages will facilitate storage, consolidation, and retrieval. For all age levels, you should model elaboration by thinking aloud. For example, you might use the fact "Australia is the smallest continent." Your elaboration might include such a thought as, "Australia looks like an island, and islands are usually smaller than continents."

Elaboration is an extremely important learning and memory strategy that takes effort on the student's part to engage in consciously. Thus, it's important to go through all of the practice rounds in the lesson and to continue to emphasize elaboration and how to incorporate it with methods taught in subsequent lessons. During the practice exercises, help the student to elaborate by asking questions and providing cues. Students tend to say that they don't know anything about the subject. In such cases, remind the students of related information that they know and encourage them to make inferences. All students know some related information; it's just a matter of helping them understand the connections.

Because of the challenge of self-elaborating on a consistent basis, you should emphasize the asking and answering of the "why does this make sense" question. This provides the student with a structure that generalizes to all material. Answering the question will force the student to retrieve and think about related information, thereby engaging in elaboration. As the research reports, it's not necessary that student's answers to the why questions be completely correct. What's important is that the answers make sense to the student.

For Practice Round 4, the student may be overwhelmed with fact-laden paragraphs. In such instances, direct the student to select the most important new fact or the most unknown fact. The "why" question will then need to be answered for the selected fact. Presumably, the other facts in the paragraph are related, resulting in some "carryover" elaboration and helpful associations for the other facts.

At the end of the lesson, stress that elaboration is time-consuming and takes effort, but that the payoff is well worth it. Also, remind all grade levels to bring a science or social studies text to the next lesson.

Lower Level Directions

Begin by reading the Spanish terms from last time and having the student respond orally. Then, tally the number correct and discuss the benefits of creating and using study cards. Next, using some study cards, have the student explain and demonstrate how to properly use the cards, following the rules in Lesson 29. Reteach and practice any procedures the student is not following correctly.

Lesson 31: Remembering What You Read

You will not find the Preview, Read, Select, Answer, and Review (PRSAR, lower level), or Preview, Elaborate, Read, Select, Answer, and Review (PERSAR, upper level) strategy cited in research literature because it is a combination of elaboration and the evidence-based PQRST strategy. In this workbook, the PQRST strategy has been adapted and incorporated with elaboration to make it more age appropriate and effective for textbook material. The upper level strategy consists of two rounds of elaboration, whereas the lower level has only one. A science or social studies textbook should be used in order to adequately practice the "preview" and "review" steps.

During future practice rounds, it's not necessary for the students to write anything down, but you should have them think aloud so that you can verify that they are correctly applying each step. Even after a few rounds of practice, students are unlikely to continue using this systematic approach to reading textbooks without constant encouragement and reminders. When students do report using the strategy, try to collect their classroom test scores on the material and attribute improved performance to the use of this strategy.

Lower Level Directions

For the "Review" section, ask a simple, direct question about each fact studied during the last lesson (including those the student selected from a reading). Have the student respond orally and keep a tally of the correct responses. There are too few facts to validly compare the recall of Practice Round 1 with recall for the facts that were elaborated. Rather, stress how well thinking about the information and answering the "why" question can support memory for new and difficult facts.

Upper Level Directions

If the student has difficulty with outright recall of the facts studied during Lesson 30, ask a direct question about each fact. When finished with the review, emphasize how well some rather difficult facts were remembered because of elaboration.

Lesson 32: Creating and Using Review Sheets

Assist the student with creating a review sheet. For many students, the most challenging aspect is deciding which facts to include in the review. In general, the most important facts, and those that are the most difficult to understand and learn, should be included. You might need to explain to students that not every fact needs to be included on a review sheet; related information will be remembered well even if it's not specifically listed.

Creating a review sheet is a basic study skill. Following this lesson's rules for studying from a review sheet is where the memory strategies come into play. The sheet should always be used in a self-testing mode (see Lesson 33) and the more difficult items studied longer (like sorting study cards in Lesson 29). A blank review sheet can be found in Appendix L.

If the student needs to generate a review sheet for a class, require the student to bring in the appropriate textbook or to create the sheet outside of the memory training sessions. If you choose the latter alternative, have the student show you what he or she created and practice using it correctly. Later, ask the student how well he or she scored when tested on the material.

Lower Level Directions

Younger students will usually need assistance selecting the best facts to include on the review sheet. Additionally, they may need help formulating relevant questions. Immediately after they complete the lesson's practice sheet, have them practice using the sheet correctly.

Upper Level Directions

Most teachers provide students with study guides or review packets. Thus, it's important to discuss the "How to Study From a Teacher's Review Sheet" section with the student. It's also recommended that you have the student apply these tips, using an actual teacher's study guide or review packet.

Lesson 33: Testing Yourself

The powerful "testing effect" works for several reasons. The primary reason is that testing forces the student to actually retrieve the information, thereby strengthening the pathways and consolidating information. Another reason is that following a testing format during study means that the real test's questions and format are more likely to serve as retrieval cues. Furthermore, older students will often go back and review information they couldn't recall when self-testing. Make sure that students follow the rules or tips as they demonstrate the procedures for you.

Lesson 34: Study Skills That Help Memory

Most memory strategies are consistent with effective study skills. This lesson highlights some study skills that are especially supportive of memory functions.

Lower Level Directions

Discuss the recommendations with the student. For those items the student checks, verify that the student is applying the practice appropriately. Then have the student commit to trying two new study skills and reporting back to you on the results of his or her efforts.

Upper Level Directions

For the "Review" section, ask direct questions about the facts the student recorded during Lesson 31. Compare the responses for Practice Round 1 and the PERSAR method. Discuss the potential effectiveness of PERSAR and encourage the student to keep on using it outside of the training sessions.

Lesson 35: Using Music to Remember

To help younger children and challenged students understand the arrangement of the heart's chambers, you could show them the online image of the heart found on the Wikipedia Web site at http://en.wikipedia.org/wiki/Heart, or you might draw a simple four-chambered heart. Then assist them with creating simple lyrics that contain all the necessary facts. You can help develop the song as much as necessary because songs are just as memorable when someone else creates them.

Lesson 36: Review and Reflections

Have the student complete the responses the best that he or she can before providing any prompts or cues. After the student has finished responding, provide immediate corrective feedback. The student's responses will allow you to determine how well he or she understands the rationale for and benefit of the strategies. The responses will also indicate whether additional review and practice is needed for the rules and procedures.

Lesson 37: Remembering to Do Things

This is the first of three lessons intended primarily for children and adolescents with severe memory problems. The purpose of the lesson is to help the trainee develop planning skills that will allow more independent daily functioning. The lesson is not about getting homework done on time or studying in advance for tests. Rather, it's more about the challenges of daily living in the home environment—what are referred to as "everyday memory problems."

Before doing Practice Round 2, have the student commit to trying a new method of remembering to do things. Discuss the details of how the student will implement the new procedure, and, during future lessons, monitor his or her use of the procedure.

Practice Round 2 gives you the first opportunity to train the student to properly plan and enter dates and times for all upcoming events, plans, and obligations. Make sure he or she enters the actual times of the events under the selected date. Also, teach the student to enter all aspects of accomplishing a particular goal. For example, if he or she is planning to attend a special event that requires advance purchase of tickets, then a date for purchasing the tickets needs to be entered in addition to the time and date of the event.

Once the student has completed Practice Round 2 properly, have the student do this for his or her actual events. If the student did not bring a calendar, create a calendar for the month and help the student with the entries. Then assign the student to transfer these entries to his or her personal calendar. Most importantly, require the student to bring his or her appointment calendar or electronic device to all remaining memory sessions.

At the beginning of each remaining lesson, review the calendar entries with the student. During each lesson, encourage the student to carry this calendar at all times and to consult it several times per day. It's also recommended that you check with parents to determine how well the student is using the calendar independently. Also, when talking with parents, encourage them to allow the student to take responsibility for meeting obligations on time. Reinforce the student for correctly entering information into the calendar on a daily basis, and further reinforce the student whenever you have evidence that the student is checking the calendar frequently throughout the day.

Lesson 38: Memory Aids

This is a short but important lesson connected with Lessons 37 and 39 that encourages the student to use memory aids in addition to a calendar. Explain each memory aid to the student before he or she selects one (in addition to a calendar) that he or she would like to start using. Then, help the student develop and write out a detailed plan for using the memory aid. With older memory-impaired students, attempt to monitor their use of the new memory aid during future lessons. Lesson 39 will encourage the student to incorporate several of these aids into a "memory book."

Here are some explanations of and tips for using some of the aids:

➤ There are many different electronic devices, such as mobile phones, that have alarms that could be used as reminders. If the student selects this as a new option, teach the student how to fully use the device.

➤ In contrast to a "to-do list," "checklists" refer to a list of steps or procedures that need to be completed on a regular basis. These are usually for procedures that are difficult to remember and in which each step needs to be completed correctly—for example, a checklist for accessing and running an internet computer program.

➤ A memory journal is sort of a memory diary for recording daily memory successes and failures, along with the associated thoughts and feelings. It may be especially helpful in cases of traumatic brain injury where there has been a substantial decline in memory performance.

➤ A memory notebook is essentially the same as a "memory book" (see Lesson 39). It may contain a variety of information that needs to be remembered.

➤ A "memory spot" is a special designated spot in the home, such as a table, where objects and notes are placed. For example, items that need to be taken to school should be placed in the memory spot and reminder notes can also be left there. Both the student and the parents can add materials to the memory spot.

Lower Level Directions

Because the lower and upper level materials for this lesson are identical, the lesson is only printed at the upper level. Lower level students should complete this lesson.

Lesson 39: Creating and Using a Memory Book

For students who would benefit from a memory book, help them design and organize one. During future lessons, review their memory book entries and encourage them to keep using it on a daily basis. For those students who might be embarrassed to carry an actual "memory book," you might teach them how to develop and use a memory book on a laptop computer or a personal digital assistant.

Lesson 40: Plans for Using Memory Strategies (Lower Level Only)

Allow the student to complete the plan independently before having a discussion and making suggestions. For younger students and those with significant memory impairments, it is recommended that you write up a plan for the student, with details on how to use each strategy the student has decided to adopt. Copies of this plan should be shared with the student's parents and teachers. Also, the written plan can be referred to in the event that you have follow-up meetings with the student to assess future use and effectiveness of the strategies learned through this memory training program.

Lesson 40: Keyword (Upper Level Only)

The keyword procedures are fully described on the student's pages. The student needs to follow all of the steps correctly in order for keyword to be effective. The first challenge for some students is thinking of a keyword. Before suggesting a keyword that the stimulus word reminds you of, remind the student that only the first part of the stimulus word needs to match, such as the keyword "mad" for Madison. Like other visual mnemonics, the image should be interactive, funny, or bizarre. The image should also be focused on the keyword and the meaning. As the student describes the images, have the student alter them until they meet these criteria. At times, you might need to suggest an idea for an image, but let the student finish constructing it so that the image becomes his or her own. When practicing with the state capitals, a keyword should be created for both the state and the capital. With two keywords, the image can be retrieved regardless of how the question is worded.

If the student has taken Spanish and knows some of the Spanish terms provided here, use different Spanish terms or switch to French (see Appendix C). For additional practice of keyword, these materials are in the Appendices: Spanish vocabulary, French vocabulary, English vocabulary, and state capitals. If the student has vocabulary to memorize for a class, such as science vocabulary, that material is preferable. To determine the effectiveness of keyword for the student, test the student's recall after appropriate intervals, such as a couple of days or a week.

Lesson 41: Taking Class Notes

The use of abbreviations and codes is especially recommended for students with working memory deficits. Such individuals who are required to take notes should learn some basic shorthand (see Appendix J). Students with disabilities who have a note-taker or are provided with notes should still be encouraged to write down key points and thoughts as they listen to instruction.

Note-Taking Exercise

Read the "lecture" below as if you were giving a talk on the subject, emphasizing important details, and slowing down when providing lists. You may also pause for students who write slowly.

When preparing for a wilderness canoe trip, purchasing the most efficient materials, gathering safety equipment, and packing the correct amounts of high-energy foods are the three most important things to consider. The wilderness can be a dangerous environment, especially when one is traveling by water. Paddling a canoe all day or carrying a canoe and supplies across a portage can be exhausting. Thus, the first rule that all equipment must meet is that it be lightweight. When it comes to purchasing a lightweight canoe, there are many options. The best canoe would be one that is lightweight and strong at the same time. Next on the equipment list are the paddles. Paddles that are bent are more efficient, but they also need to be lightweight. The canoeist will lift the paddle thousands of times in one day. So, if the paddle weighs a pound more than it needs to, the canoeist will lift thousands of pounds more per day than necessary. Weight is also a major thing to consider when purchasing the camping equipment. Strong but lightweight backpacks, tents, and sleeping bags are a must. Clothing also needs to be efficient. With clothing, the concern is that it be suitable for many kinds of weather, rather than just being lightweight.

A canoeist who does not purchase efficient and lightweight equipment may survive the trip. He or she will just have to work harder at traveling by canoe. However, survival does depend on having all of the necessary safety equipment. Life jackets and a first-aid kit are obvious, even for newcomers. But just as important, one doesn't want to get lost in the wilderness or accidently get drawn over a dam or waterfall. So, good maps that are waterproofed are a must, regardless of whether or not one carries a GPS device. Even if cell phone coverage is available, calling 911 in an emergency does not guarantee timely assistance. The canoeist needs to plan for potential accidents and emergencies. For example, a weather radio can warn the canoeist of potentially dangerous weather.

Finally, all food needed for the duration of the trip needs to be purchased. Every meal should be carefully planned so that just the right amount of food is brought along. First and foremost, the food needs to be lightweight. This is accomplished by purchasing dehydrated foods (dried foods with no water left in them). For example, a bag of rice is more efficient than canned foods that contain liquid. Second, the canoeist should bring some high energy foods, such as candy bars. Ways of protecting the food also are important. All food needs to be in waterproof containers, and a method of protecting the food from wild animals also needs to be considered. Wilderness campers usually protect food from animals by dangling a food bag on rope that has been thrown over a tree branch. Regarding drinking water, the ideal situation is when the canoeist can use water from the lakes or rivers being paddled. Special kits for killing the germs in the water can be purchased. If the water in the environment is unusable, water can be carried along but it will quickly add a lot of weight to the canoe. An adult needs to drink about a gallon of water a day, and a gallon of water weighs eight pounds.

As you can see, it takes a lot of planning if one is to go canoeing in the wilderness. After all the necessary equipment and supplies are loaded into the canoe, there's not much room left for anything else. Luxury items can be left at home, but all of the materials discussed in this presentation, as well as some others not mentioned, are absolutely essential.

When you are finished reading the lecture, tell the student to review the notes and make changes or additions. Then, examine the student's notes for completeness and efficiency. If the student did not make any abbreviations or coded words while taking notes, suggest some that could have been used for words that were frequently repeated, such as "lightweight" or "emergency." If the student tried to write verbatim notes, demonstrate how to paraphrase and write key phrases and terms instead of entire sentences. After this discussion, have the student read the steps under the "Reviewing, Editing, and Adding" section and then have the student complete steps 3–5. End the session by encouraging the student to adopt these new note-taking methods, and require the student to bring class notes to future memory lessons so that you can review his or her notes and make suggestions.

Lesson 42: Studying From Class Notes

Using notes from one of the student's classes, have the student practice the procedures in the "How to Study From Class Notes" section. Converting the notes into study cards or a review sheet is perhaps the most important procedure (see the "Practice" section). Even students who are skilled note-takers should practice and demonstrate these study procedures at least three times during memory sessions. Ideally, you should follow up at periodic intervals to encourage the student to maintain these memory enhancing study skills. At the end of the session, ask the student to bring his or her assignment calendar or notebook to the next training session.

Lesson 43: Scheduling Reviews

To test the student's recall with keyword, go back to the vocabulary and capitals in Lesson 40. As you read the terms or states, accept oral responses and keep a tally of the number correct. If the student's recall is better when using keyword, discuss the implications and potential applications.

Regarding distributed reviews, also known as spaced reviews or expanding interval reviews, the text on the student's pages explains the evidence-based recommendations. The most important concept is that memory connections become stronger when it takes some effort to retrieve the information. Of course, understanding these principles is useless if the student does not begin preparing for exams at least a week in advance. If the student brought an assignment calendar, have the student enter actual review plans after completing the practice exercise. During practice, help the student understand that material for the same exam may be divided up into two or more sets of materials, with each set having its own review schedule. Continue to monitor the student's assignment calendar and compliance with planned review schedules.

Lesson 44: Teaching the Information

Discuss applications of each suggestion. Then have the student explain how he or she would do the items in the "Practice" section. If you wish to reinforce some of these practices, you may change the assignment so that the student is required to prepare some material for teaching and then teach it to you during a later training session.

Lesson 45: Using Context Cues

Help the student understand that context cues are stored in our personal memory system and knowledge is stored in our factual memory system, but the two are connected. Thus, remembering context cues can facilitate the recall of knowledge, especially when that knowledge was just learned recently. After completing the practice, discuss courses and exams where this approach might be helpful.

Lesson 46: Improving Recall During Tests

For some students, you might need to review the distinction between storage and retrieval and the idea that we often struggle to retrieve information that we actually know and still have in memory storage. After discussing all of the suggestions with the student, give the student an opportunity to apply them during the "Practice" section. The answers to the practice questions can be found in Lesson 30. After the student is finished responding, have the student report on the strategies he or she was using to improve retrieval. End the session with encouragement to try these strategies during future classroom exams, and have the student report back on the use of these strategies.

Lesson 47: Selecting, Modifying, and Combining Strategies

Students who are able to select correct strategies for the task at hand and who are able to successfully modify and combine strategies have reached the highest level of strategy use. Reaching such a high level depends on adequate development of metamemory. Simply learning how to perform a strategy is insufficient. Thus, one purpose of this lesson is to assess the progression of the student's metamemory since the beginning of the memory training. The other purpose is to provide the student with some advanced guidance in strategy selection and combination. After the student suggests pairings in Practice Round 1, suggest some of your own pairings.

Here are some answers to the items in Practice Round 2 (other strategies may also be applicable):

1. You must memorize information from material you read on your own.
    Elaboration, PERSAR, creating a review sheet
2. You have to learn some foreign language vocabulary.
    Flashcards, keyword
3. You need to remember a shopping list and you have no paper on which to write it.
    Pegword
4. You want to remember a literature selection for a quiz tomorrow.
    Imagining yourself in the scene
5. You need to memorize the spelling of some words.
    Repetition of chunks
6. You need to prepare for a final exam that covers a few chapters.
    Creating review sheets, scheduling reviews

After completing these selections, have a discussion with the student about what to do when the first approach does not work, such as using a different strategy, modifying the strategy, or combining it with another method.

Lesson 48: Test on Memory and Strategies

After the student completes the test, provide corrective feedback on any incorrect responses. If the student has no recollection of an important point, go back to the lesson with that information and review the material. The lesson in which the answer can be found is indicated after each question.

Lesson 49: Plans for Using Memory Strategies

Allow the student to complete the plan independently before having a discussion and making suggestions. For younger students and those with significant memory impairments, it is recommended that you write up a plan for the student, with details on how to use each strategy the student has decided to adopt. Copies of this plan should be shared with the student's parents and teachers. Also, the written plan can be referred to in the event that you have follow-up meetings with the student to assess future use and effectiveness of the strategies learned through this memory training program.

Lesson 50: Evaluation of Training

The purpose of this lesson is to obtain and document the student's perspective on the value of the memory training program. To avoid biasing responses, do not discuss items until the student has completed the evaluation in writing. Insightful comments that could be used to improve the workbook or any aspect of the training program may be emailed to the author at mdehn2@msn.com.

LOWER LEVEL WORKBOOK

1 Introduction for Students

Do you often forget things you wish you could remember, such as how to spell a word, where you put something, or the directions you were supposed to follow? You know that it's impossible to remember everything, no matter how hard you try. Forgetting facts and all sorts of information happens to everyone. No matter how quickly we first learn new facts, we begin forgetting at least some of them immediately after we stop trying to learn and remember them. As minutes and hours go by, forgetting happens quickly. Then, after a day or two, forgetting begins to slow down. The graphs "How Quickly People Learn" and "How Quickly People Forget" show how quickly most people learn and then forget a list of words.

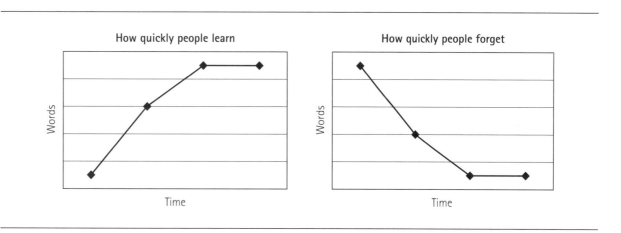

The good news is that we can learn ways to remember more and forget less. The purpose of this workbook is to help you learn methods for improving your memory. In order to learn these methods well, you will need to practice them with your memory "trainer" and use them when you study and in other situations where you need to remember things.

Learning and remembering is a big part of what our brains do. One part of the brain—let's call it the *memory center*—creates memories (see the picture titled "The Brain's Memory Center and Storage Areas"). Other parts of the brain store memories. The front part of the brain does not create or store memories, but it is responsible for using special methods or *strategies* that help us remember. Some memories aren't put into storage very well, and they don't last. Also, some memories remain in storage just fine, but we can't

The brain's memory center and storage areas

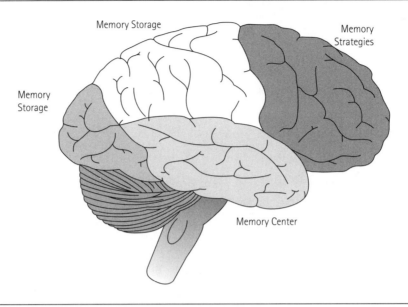

Adapted from: *Neuropsychological Perspectives on Learning Disabilities in an Era of RTI: Recommendations for Diagnosis and Intervention,* by E. Fletcher-Janzen and C. R. Reynolds (Eds.), 2008, Hoboken, NJ: Wiley. Used with permission.

remember them when we want to, such as when we forget someone's name. How well our memory works depends a lot on our memory center. Some people are born with a weaker memory center, and some people experience things that damage their memory center. For example, a serious illness or a head injury can damage the memory center.

2 Thoughts and Feelings About Memory

Name _____ Grade _____ Date _____

Directions

Discuss each answer with your trainer before writing it.

1. How is your memory for what is taught in class? Do you remember most of what is taught, or do you forget most of it?

2. How is your memory for what you try to learn on your own at school? Do you remember most of it or forget most of it?

3. How is your memory for what you need to remember at home, such as where you put things? Is it strong or weak?

4. How is your memory for things that happen to you? Is it strong or weak?

5. How often do you feel bad or get frustrated because you can't remember something? Is it never, sometimes, very often?

6. For about how long can people remember something like a new phone number in their short-term memory?

7. There are different types of long-term memory. What do you think these types might be?

8. What are some things you think you can do to make your memories last longer?

9. What are some things you don't understand about memory?

10. If you could change one thing about your memory, what would you change?

11. Discuss with your trainer any other thoughts and feelings you have about your memory, then write them down here.

12. What questions do you have about memory and how it works?

3 How Memory Works

People have two main kinds of memory: *short-term* memory and *long-term* memory.

Short-Term Memory

Everything we see and hear goes into our short-term memory before it goes into our long-term memory. What you are thinking about right now is in your short-term memory. Information only stays in short-term memory for a few seconds, 15 seconds at most. But we can keep information in short-term memory longer if we keep repeating it. There is also a limit on how much information we can hold in short-term memory. The usual limit for an elementary student is four to five pieces of information, such as five words. There are two types of short-term memory. Things we hear go into one type of short-term memory and things we see go into the other type.

Your trainer will now read you a list of five words. Immediately repeat them back. You have just put your short-term memory to work.

Long-Term Memory

Anything we remember for more than 15 seconds has made it into our long-term memory. Although some long-term memories can last a lifetime, we forget most details and newly learned facts within a few days, unless we do things to create long-lasting memories. For example, we can remember most of the details of what happened at school today, but a week from now, we will not remember nearly as much.

Like short-term memory, long-term memory can be divided into memory for what we see and memory for what we hear. Also, there are personal memories for what happens in our daily lives and memories for facts and knowledge that we must learn for school, such as arithmetic facts. We usually don't have to make a special effort to get personal experiences into memory; they go into memory automatically. But we do need to make a special effort to get facts into memory. That's why we usually have to study facts several times before they stick in our long-term memory.

Now tell your trainer the words she or he read to you a couple minutes ago. The ones you still remember are now coming out of your long-term memory, not your short-term memory.

How Things Move Through Memory

When we experience something or try to memorize facts, our short-term memory gets involved first. Then, some of the information goes from our short-term into our long-term memory. There are three steps to a long-term memory: getting it in, keeping it there, and getting it back out. When we have memory problems, the problem can happen at any step. Sometimes we cannot remember something because it never got into long-term memory; other times we cannot keep information in memory very well; and sometimes we cannot get the information back out when we want to, even though it is still stored in our memory.

Now, look at the picture of the movement of information through different kinds of memory and discuss the different kinds of memory and memory steps with your trainer.

The Movement of Information Through Different Kinds of Memory

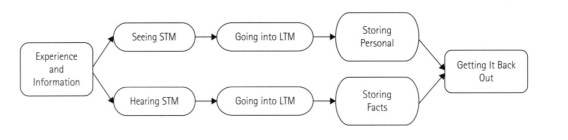

STM = Short-Term Memory and LTM = Long-Term Memory

Memory Quiz

Name _____ Grade _____ Date _____

Directions

Answer the following questions without help from your trainer. You may look back at the information presented in this lesson.

1. Unless we repeat information over and over, how long does it usually remain in short-term memory?

2. How many pieces of information can short-term memory usually hold at a time?

3. What are the two types of short-term memory?

4. When we still remember something after a minute, which kind of memory is the information coming from?

5 Is our memory for facts a different kind of memory than our memory for personal experiences?

6. Are there different reasons why people can't remember things?

7. What are the three main steps a memory goes through?

4 Memory Strengths and Weaknesses

Name _____ Grade _____ Date _____

1. With your trainer's help, list the kinds of things that you remember well.

2. With your trainer's help, list the kinds of things that you have difficulty remembering.

3. Which is easier for you to remember: words or pictures?

4. Tell your trainer about a time you forgot something and it made you feel bad.

Look at the picture below and discuss with your trainer which kinds of memory are your strengths and which kinds are weaknesses. After the two of you agree on your strengths and weaknesses, color in each part of the picture, with green for strengths and red for weaknesses.

My Memory Strengths and Weaknesses

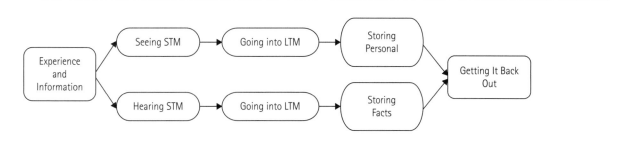

5 Memory Beliefs

Name _____ Grade _____ Date _____

Here are some statements about memory. Check the box in front of those that you believe.

❑ A person will remember something better just because he or she wants to.

❑ All memories last forever.

❑ People have no control over their memory.

❑ If you can remember something five minutes later, you will almost certainly remember it tomorrow.

❑ Repeating something over and over is the best way to create a lasting memory.

❑ People can easily tell whether they have learned something well enough to remember it tomorrow.

❑ The ability to remember things cannot be improved.

❑ Only dumb people have memory problems.

❑ If you can't remember something when someone asks you a question, it means that the information has been completely lost from your memory.

❑ How you study has nothing to do with how well you will remember the material.

❑ People will remember something better just because they are interested in it.

❑ You should spend the same amount of time trying to memorize easy material as you do for hard material.

❑ To do your best on a test, you just need to study the night before the test.

Now, ask your trainer which of the beliefs are true and discuss the ones you marked.

LESSON 6 Memorization Methods

Name _____ Grade _____ Date _____

Practice Round 1

Below is a list of six Spanish words. Let's say that you have to memorize their English meanings. Show your trainer how you will memorize them. Your trainer will provide any materials you might need.

Vaca = Cow   Ballena = Whale
Niña = Girl   Calle = Street
Perro = Dog   Sol = Sun

With your trainer's help, write a description of the method you were using to memorize the vocabulary words.

Practice Round 2

Below is a short science lesson. Imagine that you have to memorize the facts for a test. Demonstrate for your trainer how you will learn and memorize the science facts. Your trainer will provide any materials you might need.

To stay alive, you need a steady flow of blood through your body. Blood has four different parts. Each part does something different. The liquid part moves food to the body cells and takes wastes away from the cells. Red blood cells, which make blood look red, move oxygen from the lungs to the body cells. White blood cells protect the body from illness by killing germs. The last part, the sticky part, stops bleeding when there is a cut.

With your trainer's help, write a description of the method you were using to memorize the science facts.

Questions

1. Tell your trainer about any other the methods you use when you want to learn and memorize facts and information. After discussing the methods with your trainer, decide how to describe each of them in a few words and write the descriptions here.

2. Which of the above methods is your favorite?

3. If you want to remember something for a long time, which of your methods works best?

4. Do you use different methods for different kinds of material? Explain.

5. How do you know when you have studied something long enough that you will remember it?

7 Memory Strategies Survey

Name _____ Grade _____ Date _____

Below is a list of different methods that students use to memorize information. Circle the word that best describes how often you use each method. Ask your trainer about any words you don't understand.

1. Repeating the information several times · · · · · · · · · *Never* · · · *Sometimes* · · · *Always*

2. Making a list of things to do · · · · · · · · · · · · · · · · *Never* · · · *Sometimes* · · · *Always*

3. Writing information down several times · · · · · · · · · *Never* · · · *Sometimes* · · · *Always*

4. Putting the words to remember in a sentence or story · *Never* · · · *Sometimes* · · · *Always*

5. Grouping words into categories · · · · · · · · · · · · · · *Never* · · · *Sometimes* · · · *Always*

6. Using special words, such as HOMES for the names of the Great Lakes · · · · · · · · · · · · · · · · · *Never* · · · *Sometimes* · · · *Always*

7. Creating pictures in my head, such as picturing an apple when I need to remember the word "apple" · *Never* · · · *Sometimes* · · · *Always*

8. Having someone test me with flash cards · · · · · · · *Never* · · · *Sometimes* · · · *Always*

9. Reviewing or studying the same material every day for several days · · · · · · · · · · · · · · · · · *Never* · · · *Sometimes* · · · *Always*

10. Saying the names of objects I need to remember, such as saying "ball" to myself when I want to remember that I saw a ball · · · · · · · · · · · · *Never* · · · *Sometimes* · · · *Always*

11. Placing objects or notes in a special location   *Never*   *Sometimes*   *Always*

12. Stopping and thinking about new information as I hear it or read it   *Never*   *Sometimes*   *Always*

13. Asking someone to help me remember to do something   *Never*   *Sometimes*   *Always*

Goals for Improving Memory

Name _____ Grade _____ Date _____

Review Lesson 4, where you colored in your memory strengths and weaknesses. List your memory weaknesses here.

In school, what do you have the most difficulty remembering?

At home, what kinds of things do you frequently forget?

With your trainer's help, write the three most important goals that you have for improving your memory.

1.

2.

3.

Is there anything else you would like to gain from memory training? If yes, explain.

LESSON 9 A Memory Experiment

Name _____ Grade _____ Date _____

A Memory Experiment: Part I

When your trainer says "begin" try to memorize the list of words below as you read the list four times.

Cherry

Pants

Table

Potato

Desk

Gloves

Banana

Chair

Peach

Shirt

Couch

Boots

Things That Can Harm the Memory Center

Here are some things that can harm the brain's memory center:

➤ Lots of worrying

➤ Feeling really bad for long periods of time

➤ Getting hit in the head

➤ Being unable to breathe

➤ Problems controlling diabetes

➤ A high fever

➤ Drug abuse

➤ Getting very little sleep

➤ Illnesses that put you in the hospital

A Memory Experiment: Part I Continued

A few minutes ago you tried to memorize a list of 12 words. Write the words you remember below.

A Memory Experiment: Part II

This time your trainer will read a list of 12 words to you. Close your eyes as you listen. When you hear each word, picture that thing in your mind, and then tell your trainer what you see.

Things That Can Help Memory

Here are some things that help memory work better. Check the ones that you do.

❏ Organizing the information you want to remember
❏ Repeating things to yourself
❏ Studying material more than once
❏ Practicing a skill many times
❏ Testing yourself or having someone test you
❏ Making yourself remember instead of just looking at the answer
❏ Thinking about the information you are studying
❏ Taking breaks when you study
❏ Getting plenty of sleep
❏ Creating pictures of words in your mind
❏ Naming things that you see

A Memory Experiment: Part II Continued

A few minutes ago you listened to a list of 12 words that you pictured in your mind. Write the words you remember here.

Now count the number correct from Parts I and II of the experiment. On which part did you do better? Why do you think you did better on this part? Discuss this with your trainer.

Assignment

Picturing things in your mind can help you remember. This coming week, make a special effort to picture more things in your mind. Try picturing:

❏ Directions from your teacher
❏ New facts that you need to remember

10 Review and Reflections

Name _____ Grade _____ Date _____

Since you began this memory training, list some new things you have learned about how everyone's memory works.

List some new things you have learned about your own memory.

What do you think and feel about these memory training sessions?

11 Repetition

Name _____ Grade _____ Date _____

Review of the Memory Experiment

Tell your trainer about the times you've tried picturing things in your mind since the Memory Experiment lesson.

Picturing things in your mind may help you remember, because you may have a better memory for what you see than for what you hear. Also, if you picture things you hear or read, the information is stored in two kinds of memory. So, if you forget it one way, you might remember it the other way.

Practice Round 1

Your trainer will now read a list of seven words to you just once. This time, there is no need to picture them in your mind. When she or he is finished, say as many words as you can remember.

How many words did you remember?

Repetition

Repeating things over and over is a method most people use when they want to remember something for more than a few seconds. Repetition helps keep things in short-term memory, and it also helps move information into long-term memory. In everyday life, you use repetition to remember something that is not written down. For example, you might repeat a phone number several times after someone tells you the number. Or, you might repeat a list of directions from a teacher.

Practice Round 2

Your trainer will now slowly read you a list of seven shopping items to remember. When you hear the first word, keep whispering it until you hear the second word, then add the second word, and then keep adding each new word to the list as you hear it. For example, if the words are "apple, lettuce, plates," keep repeating "apple" until you hear "lettuce," then say "apple, lettuce" until you hear "plates," and then keep saying "apple, lettuce, plates." Now, practice three other words with your trainer.

Now use this method, adding words to the list as your hear them, as your trainer says seven words. When she or he is finished, say as many words as you can remember.

How many words did you remember?

Did you remember more words this time than in Practice Round 1?

Do you think this kind of repetition helps your short-term memory?

12 Repeating Written Information

Name _____ Grade _____ Date _____

Repeating information is also helpful when you want to memorize something that is in writing. Repeating written information is a little different than repeating what you hear. When the words are in writing, just read through the entire list instead of adding one word at a time to what you are repeating. When you go over the list repeatedly, be sure to actually whisper the words to yourself, instead of just reading them silently.

Practice Round 1

Whisper the words below as you repeat the list several times. Keep repeating the words until you think you know them all. After you've finished, cover the words and immediately write down as many as you can remember.

<u>Write words here</u>

Drum
Coat
Fire
Train
Wall
Game
Doll
Clock
Foot
Ring

Practice Round 2

Writing things over and over is another way of getting them into memory. On a separate piece of paper, write each of the following words five times.

| Bottle | Heart | Rabbit | Truck | Donkey |
| Cloud | Pants | Dress | Swing | Horse |

Practice Round 2 Continued

Now write as many words as you can remember here:

Look at how many you had correct for each practice round. Which method works better for you: saying the words to yourself or copying the words?

Do you think you could do even better if you say them to yourself as you write them down?

Assignment

Practice using the repetition method whenever someone says something to you that you need to remember. Also, try using written repetition when you need to memorize words, such as vocabulary words, for school.

For the next memory training session, bring your spelling book.

13 Using Repetition to Study Spelling

Many students practice spelling by copying the words or by spelling them aloud. You might remember spelling even better if you combine repetition and writing when you practice the words. Let's use the word "monkey" to practice the steps below. Do each step before going to the next one.

1. Say the word. Then spell it aloud as you point to each letter with a pencil.
2. Copy the word, saying each letter aloud as you print it.
3. Look at the word you printed. Say the word and spell it aloud as you point to each letter with your pencil.
4. Cover up the word and spell it aloud. Check to see if you spelled it correctly. If not, repeat all the steps.

Now use this method to practice your spelling words for this week.

14 Chunking

Name _____ Grade _____ Date _____

Imagine that you want to remember someone's phone number. Say this phone number aloud one number at a time: 5 1 2 3 9 7 4 8 0 6

Now cover up the phone number and say it.

When we want to remember things, like number and letters, it helps to put them into small groups called *chunks*. This time, put the numbers together into chunks of two. For example, for 5, 1, say "fifty-one." Try chunking this phone number:

4 7 1 9 7 3 2 5 7 6

Now cover up the phone number and say it. Did you remember the phone number better this time?

Continue chunking the phone numbers below with your trainer. After you have chunked each number, cover it up and recall it. After a round of putting the numbers in chunks of two, try putting them into chunks of three with the last number by itself.

5 7 8 3 7 2 9 9 1 0   9 8 3 4 5 2 3 1 7 6

7 0 1 4 8 6 3 2 0 9   4 8 5 9 7 3 1 2 6 0

5 9 3 4 8 1 3 3 7 2   3 9 1 4 5 8 2 7 0 6

Combining Repetition and Chunking

Sometimes, you can combine two different memory methods. This can help you remember things even better. This time after you chunk the phone number, repeat the chunks a few times. For example, for 6 7 1 9 7 3 2 5 7 4, you will repeat 67, 19, 73, 25, 74 a few times. Practice this combined method on the numbers above.

Chunking and Repeating Words

Now try chunking words by putting the words you want to memorize in groups of three. After you repeat a group of three several times, go on to the next group of three until you finish the list. Use these words for practice:

Hammer Ball Car	Apple Hat Lion
Carrot Mouse Tree	Church Phone Boat

How do you feel about chunking? Does it seem to help you remember more?

15 Review of Repetition and Chunking

Name _____ Grade _____ Date _____

Review

1. Explain how you should repeat words to yourself when you are trying to memorize a list you are listening to.

2. When you are repeating a written list, explain how you should do it.

3. Explain how to chunk information.

Repetition Practice

Practice the repetition method with the words below without chunking. Then cover them up and write as many as you can.

<u>Write the words here</u>

Winter
Tunnel
Dream
Wheat
Hotel
Creek
Office
Tiger
Lamp

More Practice With Combining Repetition and Chunking

Now try to remember the list of nine shopping items below. Put them in chunks of three and say each chunk several times. Then cover up the list and write the words you can remember on a separate piece of paper.

Glue   Nails   Butter   Paper   Grapes   Comb   Soap   Folder   Water

How many did you remember?

Which works better for you: repetition alone or repetition and chunking combined?

16 Using Chunking to Memorize Spelling

Name _____ Grade _____ Date _____

Chunking can help you remember how to spell words. First, you must divide the words into syllables. Do this by drawing a line between the syllables, like this: sun/set. Second, say the letters in each chunk together, pausing before you do another chunk. For example, say "s-u-n," then pause and say "s-e-t."

Practice

Try chunking with the following spelling words. First draw lines between the syllables. Then say the letters in syllable chunks. After spelling each word this way three times, cover up the list and write them on the right.

<u>Spell the words here</u>

Carpet
Window
Computer
Sensation
Wonderful
Retirement

Now use this method to practice your spelling words for this week.

Thoughts About Memory Training

From practicing repetition and chunking, what new things have you learned about how your memory works?

Do you think these methods help improve your memory? If yes, how do they help?

17 Putting Words Into Sentences and Stories

Name _____ Grade _____ Date _____

Repetition and Chunking Practice

Combine the repetition and chunking methods as you go over the list of words below. Keep going over them until you think you have them memorized. Then cover the words and say them.

Cabbage   Umbrella   Spider   Violin   Basket   Saddle

Putting Words in Sentences

Another way to remember a word is to put it into a sentence. For example, the word "bananas" is easier to remember when it is in the sentence, "Monkeys love bananas."

Practice

For each word on the shopping list below, create and write a short sentence that includes the word.

Write the sentences here

Turkey

Peanuts

Flower

Backpack

Toothpaste

Baseball

Now cover up the words and sentences and write the words below. First, try to remember each sentence that you wrote. Then "pull out" each word you need to remember and write it here.

Putting the Words Into a Story

Another way to remember words is to put them into a story. When you recall the story, you will recognize the words you want to remember.

Practice

Make up a short story using the words below. First think of what the story is going to be about, and tell your trainer the idea of your story. Then write the story and include each of the words. Try to make the story funny and it will be easier to remember.

Airplane   Tomato   Rope   Pancakes   Wheels   Gloves

Write the story here. Each sentence should have at least one of the words in it. The words do not need to be used in order.

Now cover up the words and the story. Retell the story aloud, and as you come to each word on the list, write it here:

How do you feel about these two methods?

What kinds of information might they help you remember?

Assignment

Try using the sentences or story method with words or facts you need to remember for a science or social studies chapter. You can try this now or at a later session.

18 Comparing Memory Methods

Name _____ Grade _____ Date _____

During the last session you memorized a list of six words, using the repetition and chunking methods combined. Write the words you remember here.

During the last session you created six sentences to help you remember some words. Try to remember those sentences now and write the words here.

During the last session you also made up a story to help you remember six words. Try to remember the story now and write the words here.

With which method did you remember the most words?

19 Using Arithmetic to Build Memory

Name _____ Grade _____ Date _____

Short-term and long-term memory help you do arithmetic problems. It works the other way too. Practicing with arithmetic facts can help make your short-term memory stronger. Here's how it works. Your trainer will show you two arithmetic flash cards. Tell her or him the answer to each card, and then say the answers you gave in order. For example, when you see 5 + 2, say "7," and when you see 4 + 5, say "9." Then, when the last card is put down, say "7, 9." When this becomes easy to do, you will practice remembering three answers in a row, then four, and so on.

Now try it with some arithmetic flash cards. See if you can remember 10 pairs of answers without making any mistakes.

How did you do?

Assignment

If you have arithmetic flash cards at home you might ask a parent to do this exercise with you. Always use a set of flash cards that you already know the answers to. The arithmetic should be easy, only remembering the answers in order should be hard. Your trainer will send home directions for your parent.

20 Using Cards to Build Memory

Name _____ Grade _____ Date _____

A deck of playing cards can also be used to strengthen your short-term memory. To play, you must remember cards you have seen a certain number of cards back. For example, it works like this when you are asked to remember what you saw two cards back: If you see 6—3—4—7—5 one at a time, you would say "six" when the 4 is shown, "three" when the 7 is shown, and "four" when the 5 is shown. Let's start by having you remember the card you saw just before. When you get 10 of these correct in a row, you can go to the next level, where you will need to remember what you saw two cards before. Your trainer will keep adding another card back to remember until you hit your level of difficulty.

Now, explain to your trainer what you were doing to remember the cards. If you don't have a strategy, your trainer might suggest one.

Assignment

Ask a parent to play this memory-building game with you at home. Your trainer will send home directions for your parent.

Jesse: A True Story About Someone With Memory Problems

A 9-year-old girl we shall call Jesse had problems learning and remembering things. It all started when Jesse was a baby; she fell and hit her head so hard that she needed brain surgery. Growing up as a preschooler, Jesse could do everything that other kids her age could do but her parents did notice that she was forgetful. For example, she had a hard time remembering where things were kept or where she put things. When she started school, other memory problems began to show. Jesse had a hard time remembering teacher's directions for even a minute and would forget a lot of what she learned by the very next day.

Jesse knew she had memory problems, and she was afraid of her memory. She would get very upset whenever her parents tried to make her play memory games and when they tried to help her memorize facts for school. The summer she was nine, Jesse's parents took her to get some memory training. The first thing Jesse learned was how to repeat things to herself. This was something she had never done before. She discovered that if she repeated things she could remember more. Jesse then learned to play a game where she had to remember toys and other things that were placed on the table in front of her. She discovered that she could remember more of what she saw when she said the names of the objects to herself.

Jesse learned a few other memory methods that summer. By the end of the summer, Jesse was feeling much better about her memory. Her memory no longer scared her. She had learned that she could have some control over it.

21 Remembering Locations to Build Memory

Name _____ Grade _____ Date _____

Trying to remember what you see and where you see it can make your short-term memory stronger. In the boxes below you will see Xs and Os in certain locations. Try to remember where they are. When your trainer covers up a box, mark the Xs and Os in the correct places in the box at the right.

Fill in Xs and Os here

22 Picturing Verbal Information

Name _____ Grade _____ Date _____

Practice Round 1

You will have one minute to study the words below. Silently read through the list as many times as you can.

Castle	Nose	Spider	Frog	Truck
Phone	Camel	Rainbow	Tree	Sock

Helping Your Short-Term Memory in the Classroom

When you help your short-term memory, you will learn and remember better. Below are ways to help your short-term memory. Check the ones you already do.

❏ Keep my desk and backpack neat and organized
❏ Have the materials I need before class begins
❏ Repeat directions to myself right after the teacher says them
❏ Repeat directions to myself until I get them written down
❏ Organize information before I study it
❏ Do an assignment, activity, or project one step at a time
❏ Try to picture information I am reading or hearing

Assignment

From the list above, try something new to help your short-term memory. Next week, your trainer will ask you about what you have tried.

Practice Round 1 Continued

A few minutes ago, you tried to memorize a list of 10 words. Write the words you remember below.

Picturing What We Hear and Read

Memories of what we hear and read are called *verbal* memories. Memories of what we see are called *visual* memories. When we create pictures in our minds, they are called *images*, and these images are stored as visual memories. Images are remembered just as well as things we have actually seen. When we create images of words and sentences, we will remember that verbal information better, because it gives us another way of remembering the information. In an earlier lesson, you pictured words as they were read to you. Did you remember more words when you pictured them? Most people do.

Practice Round 2

Below is another list of words to memorize. After you read each word, close your eyes for a few seconds and create an image of that thing. Tell your trainer when you have finished going through the list.

| Baseball | Hammer | Airplane | Turkey | Carrot |
| Mouse | Flower | Snake | Bike | Piano |

Helping Your Short-Term Memory at Home

Here are some things you can do to help your short-term memory when you study or do homework at home. Check the ones that you already do.

❏ Always study in the same place
❏ Have all the materials I need, such as paper and a dictionary, in my study area
❏ Study in a quiet place where I can't hear music, a TV, or people talking
❏ Keep an example of what I have to do, such as a math problem, in front of me
❏ Keep a list of the steps I have to complete in front of me

❏ When I don't understand something, I read it again

❏ Take breaks when it becomes hard to concentrate

Assignment

From the list above, try something new to help your short-term memory. Next week, your trainer will ask you about what you have tried.

Practice Round 2 Continued

A few minutes ago you created images of 10 words. Write the words you remember here.

How many words did you remember from Practice Round 1?

How many words did you remember from Practice Round 2?

On which Practice Round did you do better?

Why do you think you did better on this Round?

Did creating images make a difference?

Visualizing Directions

Creating images, also called *visualizing*, can help you remember directions. When you hear directions, visualize what needs to be done and imagine yourself doing it. Do this for each step of the directions your trainer will now read to you.

Now describe your images for your trainer.

Were you in the scenes?

Now say all the directions in order.

Do you think visualizing helped?

Why does visualizing help you remember verbal information better? Discuss this with your trainer.

Assignment

This coming week, try to visualize all the steps in directions that your teachers or parents give you. When you do, imagine yourself doing each step.

23 Naming and Describing What You See

Name _____ Grade _____ Date _____

Practice Round 1

You will have 15 seconds to look at the shapes below.

Now draw the shapes from memory on a blank sheet of paper.

How did you do?

Practice Round 2

Naming and describing what you see helps you remember it better, because the information goes into both your verbal and visual memory. When looking at the star above, for example, you might have said to yourself, "A star with seven points." As you look at the shapes below, use words to describe them to yourself. Say your descriptions aloud so that your trainer can hear you.

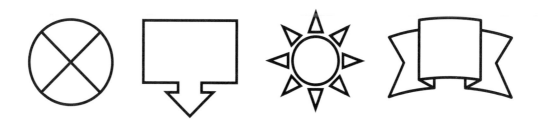

Now draw the shapes from memory on a blank sheet of paper.

Did you remember the details better this time?

Assignment

This coming week, look for situations where you need to remember something that you see and try this method of using words to describe it to yourself. At the next session, be prepared to tell your trainer about the times you tried this.

24 Grouping Words by Category

Name _____ Grade _____ Date _____

Review

Last time you looked at several figures and then drew them from memory. On a separate sheet of paper, draw the figures the best that you can, even if you can't remember all of the details.

Now draw the figures you had named and described to yourself.

Did you remember the figures you had named and described better than the others?

Practice Round 1

You will have one minute to memorize the list of words below by repeating them over and over to yourself. Cover the words when time is called.

Hammer	Carrots	Gloves	Wrench	Shoes
Cabbage	Pliers	Beans	Pajamas	

Memory Likes Organization

When the information we put into memory is organized, it is much easier to remember. That's because our memory keeps the same kinds of information together. For example, what we know about animals is kept in the same place in the brain and what we know about plants is kept in a different place. So, it's important to organize information before we try to memorize it.

Practice Round 1 Continued

Now write the words you tried to memorize here.

Practice Round 2

On a blank sheet of paper, organize the words below into categories. Write the name of each category at the top of each group. Then study the words by first memorizing the names of the categories. Then repeat the items under each category a few times before you go on to the next category. Tell your trainer when you are finished.

Table	Ship	Book	Oranges	Couch	Radio
Cherries	Bed	Newspaper	Truck	Apples	Airplane

Other Ways of Organizing Information

Putting words into categories is one way to organize information. Other ways include alphabetizing and putting things in order from first to last. Sometimes, it even helps to reorganize information that has been given to you by a teacher or that you find in a book. When you do this, organize the information in a way that makes sense to you.

Practice Round 2 Continued

Now write the words you memorized by category here.

This time there were more words to remember than in Practice Round 1. How did you do? Does organizing the information make it easier to remember?

Practice Round 3

Imagine you need to memorize the science facts below for a quiz tomorrow. On a sheet of paper, group the facts together in a way that makes sense.

> Blood moves through arteries
> Digestion begins in the stomach
> Kidneys remove waste from the body
> There are red and white blood cells
> Lungs take carbon dioxide out of the body
> The intestines finish digesting food
> Some blood cells kill germs
> Sweating allows waste to pass through the skin
> Bile helps digest food

Assignment

With your trainer, discuss the kinds of information you have to memorize for school. Talk about how you might organize or reorganize information to make it easier to remember. Come up with a plan for how you will try this method.

25 Imagining Yourself in the Scene

Name _____ Grade _____ Date _____

Review

During the last lesson, you memorized some words by repeating them. Write the words you remember here.

Now write the words that you put into four categories before memorizing them.

Now write the science facts that you organized.

Do you think putting words into groups and organizing information helps you remember it better? Why?

Using Imagination to Help You Remember

When you are listening to or reading a story, a social studies book, or any book in which something is happening, you should try to imagine yourself being there and watching the action from up close. Doing this will help you remember the facts and information later on.

Practice

As you read the story below, stop now and then and imagine yourself being there and seeing everything that is happening from up close.

Washington's Army at Valley Forge

When winter came, George Washington took his large army to a small valley called Valley Forge. The soldiers were strong and healthy when they arrived. They quickly cut down trees and built some log cabins. The winter was long and cold and wet. The men suffered terribly and many of them died before winter was over. The first problem was that they did not have warm clothing. Most of them had only ragged clothing. They were constantly cold and uncomfortable. The second problem was that there was not enough food. Occasionally, some potatoes and meat would be brought to the valley camp, but these were not enough. All of the men became very skinny, and many of them starved to death. Even hundreds of their horses starved to death during that winter. The other killer was disease. The conditions in the camp allowed diseases to spread, and there were few doctors and almost no medicines. Valley Forge will always be remembered for the cold, the misery, and all the men who died there.

When you have finished reading, think about what you saw and how you felt and share this with your trainer.

Assignment

Try this method whenever you read social studies, science, or literature. When you take a test on what you have read, stop and imagine yourself being in that scene again. Think about what you saw and felt. This will help you remember the facts better.

26 Using Locations to Remember Information

Name _____ Grade _____ Date _____

Review

Last time you read a story about George Washington's army at Valley Forge. Before you tell your trainer the answers to the questions below, imagine yourself at Valley Forge and think about what you saw when you were at the scene.

1. What did the soldiers do when they first arrived?

2. Why did the men suffer so much from the cold?

3. Who died from starvation besides the soldiers?

4. When there was food, what kind of food was it?

5. What else did the men die from?

Do you think imagining yourself in the scene helped you remember the facts better?

Using Locations to Remember

Picturing things you want to remember with objects in your bedroom will help you remember those things. It works because you can't forget the objects in your room.

Now, list six objects in your bedroom. List them in the order they appear when you go around your room to your left.

Practice

Imagine that you have to memorize a list of endangered animals (animals that might disappear from the earth) for a science quiz tomorrow. (This is a made up list; not all of these animals are endangered.) In order of your room's objects, picture each animal with an object. The image will be easier to remember if it is funny or unusual. After you create each image, describe it to your trainer.

Siberian Tigers	Blind Frogs	Fruit Bats
Rhinoceroses	Wild Ponies	Red Wolves

27 Pegword

Name _____ Grade _____ Date _____

Review

During the last lesson, you memorized a list of endangered animals by imagining each one with an object in your bedroom. Now, go through your room and picture each object. When you do, the animal you imagined with the object should appear. Then write down the animal's name below.

How well does this method of using familiar locations or objects work for you?

Pegword

Pegword is another method that can help you remember words or facts. To use this method, you must first memorize the pegwords below. Practice and review the peg-words until you can recite them three times without looking.

One is a bun
Two is a shoe
Three is a tree
Four is a door
Five is a hive (beehive)
Six is sticks
Seven is heaven
Eight is a gate
Nine is a vine
Ten is a hen

Practice Round 1

When using pegwords, create a funny image of each item on your list with one of the peg-words. For example, if want to remember "carrots," you might picture a bunch of carrots sticking out of bun. Using the pegwords in order, pair each item below with a pegword. Describe each image to your trainer.

Knife   Flower   Toothbrush   Peanuts   Napkins   Bread

Practice Round 2

Imagine that you are going Christmas shopping and want to remember to buy a gift for each of those listed below. Imagine each one with a pegword. Share the images with your trainer.

Best friend   Father   Grandmother

Family dog   Teacher   An uncle or aunt

28 Review and Reflections

Name _____ Grade _____ Date _____

Review

Recite the list of pegwords, beginning with "One is a bun." Next, use pegwords to recall the shopping list of six items. To recall the first item, think of "bun," and you should see the first item pictured with it. Continue through the pegwords and write the list here.

Now use the same method to recall the people for whom you need to buy a Christmas gift.

Review and Reflection Questions

1. How are you feeling about the memory training so far?

2. Which memory exercise or strategy do you like the most?

3. Which memory exercise or strategy is hard to do?

4. Which memory methods or strategies have you tried using at school or home?

5. Have you been more successful at remembering things? If yes, give some examples.

6. What kinds of things are you still forgetting that you wish you could remember better?

29 Using Study Cards

Name _____ Grade _____ Date _____

Study cards have a term or question written on one side and the answer written on the other side. With study cards, someone can test you or you can test yourself. Create study cards for the following Spanish terms:

Bolso = Purse	Reina = Queen	Pato = Duck
Mudar = Shed	Zapato = Shoe	Carne = Meat
Palo = Stick	Equipo = Team	Carpa = Tent

Rules for Using Study Cards

Each time you use study cards to memorize, follow these rules:

1. Mix the cards up before you start.
2. Say aloud or whisper the questions and answers to yourself.
3. Never peek at the answer or let someone tell you the answer. Always try hard to remember. Take a guess if you need to. Then turn the card over to see if you are right.
4. Put the cards you really know into a "know" pile. Keep going through the other cards until all the cards are in the "know" pile.
5. Go through the cards on at least three different days before you take the test on them.

Practice

Practice Rules 1 to 4 with the cards you just made. When you think you know all the words, put the cards down and cover up the words above. Then write the English word for each term below as your trainer reads the Spanish words to you.

How did you do? Do you like using study cards?

Assignment

If you are using study cards for something, bring them to a future memory lesson. Also, bring your social studies book to the next memory lesson.

30 Thinking About the Information

Name _____ Grade _____ Date _____

Review

Your trainer will now ask you the meaning of the Spanish words that you tried to memorize with study cards during the last lesson.

How many did you remember?

Explain to your trainer the rules for using study cards, and then demonstrate those rules with the study cards from last time or some other study cards that you have.

Practice Round 1

Below are five science facts that are probably new to you. Study them for a couple minutes, as you normally would.

➤ The world's six continents were once joined together in one big continent.
➤ Heat and pressure change dead plants into coal.
➤ Natural gas is found at the top of underground oil.
➤ The farther water falls over a dam, the more electricity it can make.
➤ An old, dying star (sun) gets bigger before it gets smaller.

Thinking About Information

Thinking about new information you are trying to learn is a powerful way of making it easier to remember. In fact, thinking about information works better than just repeating it. You should especially think about what you already know about the topic. For example, maybe you must learn some new information about George Washington. Stopping to think about what you already know about Washington will help you remember the new information better. Here are some ways to do this kind of thinking:

1. When you hear or read a new fact, stop to think about the things you already know about the subject.

2. Think about how the new information is the same or different from what you already know. Think about how well the information fits with what you already know.

3. Try to make sense out of the new information. Especially try to figure out *why* the new fact or information makes sense. You should ask and answer this question: "Why does this new fact make sense?"

Practice Round 2

Below are five social studies facts. Think about each fact or the part of each fact that is new to you. Then, tell your trainer what you already know about it.

➤ There were statues of servants in King Tut's tomb.
➤ The ancient Mexicans built pyramids that look much like Egyptian pyramids.
➤ Some of the 50,000 miles of roads built by the Romans are still used today.
➤ The English people once beheaded one of their kings.
➤ In Australia, the wide open land where almost no one lives is called the *bush*.

Practice Round 3

Below are more social studies facts. Think about each fact and ask yourself, "Why does this make sense?" Then tell your trainer the answer.

➤ The Egyptians invented the calendar that we have today.
➤ Around the world, people eat more goat meat than cow meat.
➤ Marco Polo's father made a trip to China before Marco did.
➤ Paper was invented in China.
➤ There are more Indians (Native Americans) living west of the Mississippi River than east of the Mississippi.

Practice Round 4

You can also ask and answer the "why" question when you are reading material that you need to remember. To do this, stop after you read each paragraph; pick an important new fact in that paragraph and then answer the "why" question about that fact. Practice this now with one of your school books. Write each of the five facts you select below, and then tell your trainer the answer to the "why" question for each one.

31 Remembering What You Read

Name _____ Grade _____ Date _____

Review

Your trainer will ask you some questions about the science and social studies facts from the last lesson.

Do you believe that thinking about the new facts and answering the "why" question helped you remember the facts better?

PRSAR

There is a special way of reading information that makes it easier to remember. The steps to follow when reading are known as PRSAR. The letters stand for *Preview*, *Read*, *Select*, *Answer*, and *Review*. You already learned how to *Select* and *Answer* during the last lesson.

Preview

Before you begin to read, look the selection over and:

❑ Read the title
❑ Read the words in bold print
❑ Look at the pictures and graphs and read the information under them
❑ Read any review questions at the end

Now preview today's reading selection. After you finish previewing, look at the preview list above and check the ones you did.

Read

Now read the selection, one paragraph at a time. Stop after each paragraph to complete the *Select* and *Answer* steps below.

Select

After reading each paragraph, select what you think is the most important fact.

Answer

For each fact you select, tell your trainer the answer to the "Why does this fact make sense" question.

Review

After you have finished reading the selection, look over the headings, subheadings, bolded words, pictures, and review questions again.

32 Creating and Using Review Sheets

Name _____ Grade _____ Date _____

Review

Tell your trainer what each letter in PRSAR stands for.

Since the last lesson, have your tried using this method when you read?

Review Sheets

Making and using review sheets is similar to making and using study cards.

Rules for Creating a Review Sheet

1. Create your review sheet right after the material is covered in class or as you read it. The review sheet needs to be created at least three days before the test on the material.
2. In the Question column of your review sheet, write a question for each important fact you need to know for the test.
3. Write the answer in the Answer column.
4. If it's hard to think of a question, just put a *who, what, when,* or *where* at the front of the factual statement in your book. For example, if the fact reads "Sam Houston was the first president of Texas," your question should be "*Who* was the first president of Texas?"
5. If there are many new facts to learn, pick the ones that are the hardest to understand and learn. Not every new fact needs to go on your review sheet.
6. Write the page number where you found the information in the Page Number column.

Practice Round 1

Following the rules above, create a review sheet with six questions and answers on the short science lesson below. Use the table on the next page.

To stay alive, you need a steady flow of blood through your body. The heart is the pump that keeps your blood flowing quickly through your body. You also need the right balance of different kinds of blood. Although it looks red, blood has four different parts, and only one of the parts is red. Each part does something different. The liquid part is called plasma. It moves food to the body cells and wastes away from the cells. Red blood cells, which make blood look red, move oxygen to the body cells and carbon dioxide away from the cells. White blood cells protect the body from illness by destroying germs. Platelets help stop bleeding by forming seals over cuts.

Review Sheet

Name _____ Subject/Topic _____

Dates Reviewed ____ ____ ____ ____ ____

Page Number	Question	Answer	Correct Responses					

Practice Round 2

Following the rules below, practice using your review sheet.

Rules for Using Your Review Sheet

1. At the top of the sheet, under Dates Reviewed write in the date each time you study the sheet.
2. Cover up the Answer column and only look at the answer after you have really tried to answer it. Guess if you have to.
3. Each time you get an answer correct, put a check mark in the Correct Responses column. Once you have checked an item off as correct, you don't need to review it again until the next time you study the sheet.
4. Keep going over the questions until all of them have been checked off.
5. Be sure to study the review sheet on at least three different days before a test.

At this point, which do you prefer: study cards or a review sheet?

Assignment

Make a review sheet for one of your classes and bring it to a future lesson to show your trainer.

33 Testing Yourself

Name _____ Grade _____ Date _____

Testing yourself, or having someone test you, is another way of improving your memory for what you have studied. Testing yourself is better than just repeating things. Each time you "pull" something out of your memory, it makes it easier for you to remember it the next time. Study cards and review sheets are ideal for testing yourself. To make self-testing work, follow the rules below.

1. When using a review sheet, cover up the answers.
2. Always answer the question or guess before looking at the answer.
3. When someone else is testing you, that person should tell you the correct answer when you make a mistake.
4. Try to test yourself on at least three different days before the class test.
5. Each time, keep track of the number correct so you know if you are improving.
6. When self-testing, you don't always need study cards or a review sheet. Another way to self-test is to read it, cover up, and then see if you can repeat it correctly. Students often self-test this way when they study spelling.

Practice

Use either a review sheet or a set of flash cards that you created previously to practice self-testing. Follow the rules above when you do.

34 Study Skills That Help Memory

Name _____ Grade _____ Date _____

Here are some home study skills that will improve your memory. Check the ones that you usually do.

❏ Have a snack before you begin to study. Your memory center needs a steady supply of brain food.

❏ Get some exercise before you begin to study. It will give your brain a break and make it easier to concentrate when you sit down to study.

❏ Get organized. Have all the things you need before you sit down to study.

❏ Study in a quiet place with no distractions so that you can really pay attention.

❏ Take frequent breaks to avoid overloading your memory center. Every 30 minutes, take a break for a few minutes.

❏ Think about what the new information means to you personally. For example, think about experiences you've had that involve the subject you are studying.

❏ When you have a test the next day, review the material again just before you go to sleep. If you do, your memory center will keep working with that material while you sleep.

❏ Plan for when you will study in preparation for a test. You should review the material on at least three separate days before a test. Put the review days in your assignment notebook.

❏ Compared with the easy material that you know well, always spend more time reviewing the hard material that is difficult to understand and remember.

❏ Keep on studying the hard material even after you think you know it.

❏ When you study with a family member or a friend, ask that person to test you on the material.

Assignment

Pick two new study skills and try them this coming week. Write the skills you will try below.

See if they help you remember more of what you study. Next week, give a report to your trainer on how it went.

35 Using Music to Remember

Name _____ Grade _____ Date _____

Do you like music and singing? Once you learn a song you never really forget it. That's why songs can be used to remember facts. All you have to do is take a song that you know and replace the words with facts that you want to memorize.

Practice

Below is a science lesson about the heart. Let's say that you have to memorize how the blood flows through the heart and body. Pick a song that you will use. Then write the facts in your own words so that they fit the music. You may have to change the wording a few times to make it work.

> The heart pumps blood through the whole body. The blood leaves the heart through the heart's lower, left chamber. It goes into a large artery called the aorta. The aorta is like a tree trunk and the body's blood vessels are like its branches. The smallest branches deliver blood to all of the cells in the body. The blood then follows veins to return to the heart, where it enters the heart's upper chamber on the right side. The blood then goes to the lower, right chamber. From there it flows to the lungs and back, where it enters the heart's upper chamber on the left. The blood then goes into the left, lower chamber, where the cycle starts all over again.

Which song will you use?

Write the final version of your song below and then practice singing it a few times.

36 Review and Reflections

Name _____ Grade _____ Date _____

1. Sing the song you created last time about blood circulation. Did you remember all of it?

2. What is one important thing you should do when using study cards to memorize?

3. Should thinking about the information and answering the "why" question help you remember it better than repetition?

4. On how many different days should you study from your review sheet before a test?

5. Why should testing yourself work better than repetition?

6. Write about a time your memory has been better because you used one of the new memory methods.

7. Write about a time within the last two weeks when you could not remember something you really wanted to remember.

8. Which memory methods that you have learned lately do you like the most?

37 Remembering to Do Things

Name _____ Grade _____ Date _____

Do you want to be able to remember to do things without your parents or others always reminding you? With planning and some special memory techniques, you can remember to do things without help from others.

Practice Round 1

The most common way that people remember to do things is to make a plan, write it down, carry it with them, and constantly check it until everything is finished. Imagine you are going Christmas shopping for friends. In the space below, make up an organized list of two gifts that you plan to buy for each of four friends. For each gift, also write down the store where you plan to purchase it.

Names   Gifts   Stores

Other Ways to Remember to Do Things

Check the ones that you have done.

❑ Making plans for what needs to be done

❑ Writing things down in an appointment calendar or an electronic calendar

❑ Always carrying your electronic or other calendar with you

❑ Setting a reminder alarm or message on a cell phone, computer, or similar electronic device

❑ Placing objects in a special or unusual location where you will notice them

❑ Placing objects you want to remember in the same location (known as a memory spot)

Lessons 38 and 39 will have more ideas.

Pick one of the above methods that you have not done before and write it down below. Now, discuss with your trainer how you might start using this method. Next week report to your trainer on how it went.

Practice Round 2

Students use calendars for more than remembering school assignments. Students who really want to remember things use a calendar to write down everything that is going to happen and everything they need to do. They then carry the calendar with them at all times and keep checking it throughout the day, so that they don't forget anything. For each of the events below, make up a date and time the event will occur. Then fill in the information on the one-month calendar below. Be sure to write in the times the event will occur.

❑ A friend's birthday party that you've been invited to

❑ A school game that you plan to attend

❑ Practice for a school event that you must attend on three different dates

❑ A dental appointment you have

❑ A time to go shopping for new clothes

❑ A time to call a friend

Sun	Mon	Tue	Wed	Thu	Fri	Sat
						1
2	3	4	5	6	7	8
9	10	11	12	13	14	15
16	17	18	19	20	21	22
23	24	25	26	27	28	29
30	31					

Assignment

Next time, bring the calendar or device you will be using from now on.

38 Memory Aids

This lesson is the same as the Upper Level Lesson 38. To complete it, go to Lesson 38 in the Upper Level workbook.

39 Creating and Using a Memory Book

Name _____ Grade _____ Date _____

Some people with memory problems carry a "memory book" with them all the time, so that they can enter and look up information whenever they want. A memory book is different than a calendar. Below are the different kinds of information you can put into a memory book.

1. Pictures of people, with their names and what they do written underneath.
2. Names and phone numbers of people you might want to call. Instead of arranging them alphabetically, you might arrange them by what they do. For example, you might have a coach's name under C for *coach*.
3. Step-by-step directions for things that are hard to remember. For example, you might write down the steps for using a computer program.
4. Your school schedule, so that you can check to see what comes next and when it begins and ends.
5. A list of chores that you need to do every day or week. If any of the chores are complicated, you could write down all the steps you need to do.
6. All the steps you need to follow for certain kinds of homework and projects. For example, you might have a list of steps to follow for writing assignments.
7. Descriptions of memory strategies, including all the steps involved. You might also add the types of materials and situations for which each memory strategy works best.
8. A daily journal of memory successes and failures.
9. A diary of what happened each day.

   Below, make a list of the sections that you would have in your memory book.

Assignment

Get the materials you need and organize a memory book. Put in dividers for the sections you will have. Then start entering information for each section.

40 Plans for Using Memory Strategies

Name _____ Grade _____ Date _____

Directions

Look at the list of memory strategies below and

1. Put a "+" beside the ones that work best for you.
2. Put a "–" beside the ones that do not seem to work well for you.
3. Put an "H" beside the ones that you plan to use to improve your memory at home.
4. Put an "S" beside the ones that you plan to use to improve your memory for what you need to learn and memorize for school.

_____ Repeating Information You Hear

_____ Repeating Written Information Aloud

_____ Copying Information Several Times

_____ Using Repetition to Study Spelling

_____ Chunking

_____ Using Chunking to Memorize Spelling

_____ Putting Words into Sentences and Stories

_____ Picturing Verbal Information

_____ Naming and Describing What You See

_____ Grouping Words by Category

_____ Imagining Yourself in the Scene

_____ Using Locations to Remember Information

_____ Pegword

_____ Using Study Cards

_____ Thinking About the Information

_____ Remembering What You Read (PRSAR)

_____ Creating and Using Review Sheets

_____ Testing Yourself

_____ Using Music to Remember

_____ Remembering to Do Things

_____ Memory Aids
_____ Creating and Using a Memory Book

What other plans do you have for using any of the new memory strategies that you learned?

UPPER LEVEL WORKBOOK

LESSON 1 Introduction for Students

Do you often forget things you wish you could remember, such as where you put something, the directions you need to follow, or facts that you studied for a test? You know that it's impossible to remember everything, no matter how hard you try. Forgetting facts and all sorts of information happens to everyone. No matter how easily we first learn new facts, we begin forgetting them immediately after we stop trying to learn and remember them. As minutes, hours, and days go by, we forget more and more. After a day or two, forgetting begins to slow down. The graphs "How Quickly People Learn" and "How Quickly People Forget" illustrate approximately how quickly most people learn and then forget a list of new words.

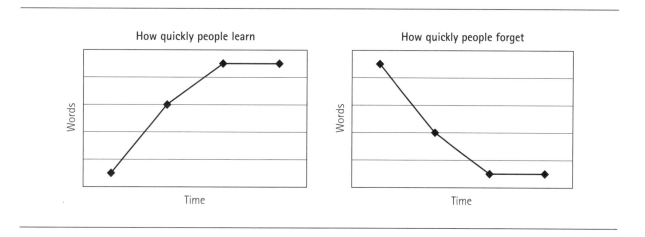

Fortunately, we can learn methods and strategies that will help us remember more and forget less. The purpose of this workbook is to help you learn methods and strategies for improving your memory. These strategies will help you learn and memorize information more efficiently and effectively when you study. That is, these strategies will allow you to make better use of the memory abilities you have. When you remember more, your learning will improve and you will do better in school. To learn these strategies well, you will need to practice them with your memory "trainer" and use them when you study and in other situations where you need to remember information.

Learning and remembering is a big part of what our brains do. Now that doctors and scientists can scan people's brains, we know a lot more about how memory works. We know where memories are kept, and we know where and how the brain creates memories that can last a long time. One part of the brain—let's call it the *memory center*—creates and stores memories; other parts of the brain store memories but don't create them; and one part of the brain neither stores nor creates them. The figure titled "The Brain's Memory Center and Storage Areas" shows the four main brain lobes. The memory center is located in the temporal lobe. The front part of the brain, known as the frontal lobe, is responsible for using strategies to help us remember, but it does not create or store memories. The parietal and occipital lobes store memories, in addition to their other jobs. Some memories aren't put into storage very well, and they don't last. Some memories remain in storage just fine, but we can't remember them when we want to, such as when we can't recall a fact that we actually know. How well our memory works depends a lot on our memory center. Some people are born with a weaker memory center, and some people experience things that damage their memory center. For example, a serious illness or a concussion can damage the memory center.

The Brain's Memory Center and Storage Areas

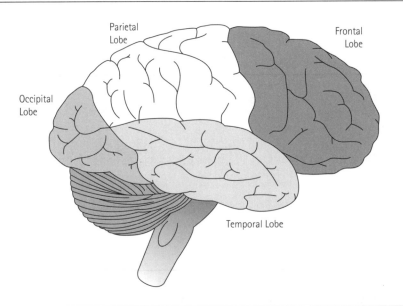

Adapted from: Neuropsychological Perspectives on Learning Disabilities in an Era of RTI: Recommendations for Diagnosis and Intervention, by E. Fletcher-Janzen and C. R. Reynolds (Eds.), 2008, Hoboken, NJ: Wiley. Used with permission.

2 Thoughts and Feelings About Memory

Name _____ Grade _____ Date _____

Directions

Discuss each response with your trainer before writing it.

1. How is your memory for what is taught in class? Do you remember most of what is taught or do you forget most of it?

2. How is your memory for material you study on your own? Do you remember most of it or forget most of it?

3. How is your memory for what you need to remember at home, such as where you put things? Is it strong or weak?

4. How is your memory for experiences and events, such as all the things you experienced yesterday? Is it strong or weak?

5. What are some things you might do differently to make your memories last longer?

6. For about how long can people remember something like a new phone number in their short-term memory?

7. There are different types of long-term memory. What do you think these types might be?

8. What do you think causes people to forget what they experience or what they study?

9. What are some things you don't understand about memory and how it works?

10. Do you ever worry about not being able to do well on a test because you won't be able to remember enough? If yes, how often?

11. How often do you feel bad or get frustrated because you can't remember something? Is it never, sometimes, or very often?

12. If you could change one thing about your memory, what would you change?

13. Discuss with your trainer any other thoughts and feelings you have about your memory. Then summarize them here.

14. What questions do you have about memory and how it works?

LESSON 3   How Memory Works

People have three main kinds of memory: *short-term* memory, *working* memory, and *long-term* memory.

Short-Term Memory

Everything we see, hear, or experience goes into our short-term memory before some of it goes into our long-term memory. When we first experience something or try to memorize something, that information is briefly held in short-term memory. Information remains in short-term memory for just a few seconds—15 seconds at the most. The only way we can keep information in short-term memory any longer is to keep repeating it. There is also a limit on how much information we can hold in short-term memory. The usual limit for an adolescent is five to seven pieces of information, such as seven words. There are two types of short-term memory: *auditory* or verbal, for information we hear, and *visual*, for what we see.

Your trainer will now read you a list of eight words. Immediately repeat them back. In trying to remember those words, you have just put your short-term memory to work.

Working Memory

What you are thinking about right now is in your working memory. Working memory is the ability to think about something and remember the details at the same time. For example, when we try to solve a math problem in our heads, we are using working memory. Or, when we try to get our ideas on to paper, we are using our working memory. When we are thinking, our working memory can only keep track of about three things at the same time. Like the other forms of memory, working memory can be divided into verbal and visual.

Your trainer will now give you a math problem to solve in your head. If you forget some of the numbers or are not able to finish the problem, it is because trying to remember the information and solve the problem at the same time overloaded your working memory. This is something that happens to everyone many times each day.

Long-Term Memory

Any experience or learning that we remember for more than 15 seconds has made it into long-term memory storage, at least temporarily. Although some long-term memories and knowledge can last a lifetime, we forget most details and newly learned facts within a few days unless we do things to create long-lasting memories. For example, we can remember most of the details of what happened at school today, but a week from now we will not remember nearly as much.

Like other types of memory, long-term memories are usually stored as either visual or verbal memories. There are also two major long-term memory storage systems. The first is the memory system that stores our personal experiences. This system records our experiences automatically. The second system stores factual knowledge that we have learned, such as knowing that George Washington was the first U.S. president. We usually have to make a conscious effort to get factual knowledge into long-term memory. That's why we have to study facts several times before they stay in long-term memory. Now tell your trainer the words she or he read to you a couple minutes ago. The ones you still remember are now coming out of your long-term memory, not your short-term memory.

The Flow of Information Through Memory

When we experience something or try to memorize information, it first enters our short-term memory. Then, some of the information goes from our short-term into our long-term memory. The process of getting something into long-term memory is called *encoding*. Information then remains in long-term *storage* for varying lengths of time. When we remember something, we are pulling it out of storage. This process is called *retrieval*. When we have memory problems, the loss of information can occur at any stage. Sometimes we can't remember information because it was never encoded, sometimes because the information did not remain in storage, and sometimes because we can't retrieve it, even though it's still in storage.

Now look at the figure titled "The Flow of Information Through Different Kinds of Memory," and then discuss the different kinds of memory and memory processes with your trainer.

The Flow of Information Through Different Kinds of Memory

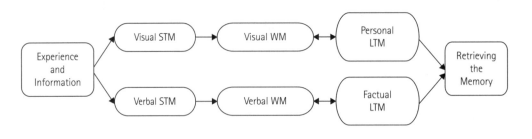

STM = Short-Term Memory, WM = Working Memory, and LTM = Long-Term Memory

Name _____ Grade _____ Date _____

Memory Quiz

Directions

Answer the following questions without help from your trainer. You may look at the figure or at the written information on memory.

1. Unless we repeat information over and over, how long does it usually remain in short-term memory?

2. How many pieces of information can short-term memory usually hold at time?

3. What are the two types of short-term memory?

4. Does everything that is in short-term memory make it into long-term memory?

5. When we can't remember what we were going to write, which kind of memory has failed?

6. How is working memory different from short-term memory?

7. What are the two main long-term memory storage systems (not visual or verbal)?

8. What does encoding mean?

9. What is retrieval?

10. Are there different reasons for why people can't remember things? Give an example.

11. You have just read the definition of a new science vocabulary term when you stop to read a text message that just came in. After taking a minute to read the message, you still remember the definition of the new word. From which memory system did you actually recall the meaning of the word: short-term, working, or long-term?

Kim: A True Story About Someone With Memory Problems

An adolescent we shall call Kim was an average student in school, but she was unhappy, because no matter how hard she studied, she could not get better grades, mainly because she did not do well on tests. Kim actually studied a lot for tests, but could not remember enough information during the test.

Some of Kim's teachers thought she did poorly on tests because she was lazy. They didn't know how hard Kim always studied for tests. If you told Kim's teachers that she had a problem remembering information, they probably wouldn't believe you, because Kim remembered the information during class as well as anyone.

A psychologist who tested Kim figured out the puzzle. Kim did have a normal short-term memory, and her long-term memory for things she learned during the day was also normal. However, overnight and during the week, Kim forgot more information than most people do. No matter how hard she tried, most things she memorized did not remain stored in her long-term memory very well. So when she couldn't remember the information during a test, it really was forgotten, even though she had remembered it for a while. (Kim's story will continue later).

4 Memory Strengths and Weaknesses

Name _____ Grade _____ Date _____

1. List the kinds of experiences and information that you remember very well.

2. List the kinds of information that you have difficulty remembering.

3. Which do you remember better: daily experiences or facts you have to learn for school?

4. Which do you remember better: things you see or things you hear?

5. Tell your trainer about a time you forgot something that you really wanted to remember.

You and your trainer should now discuss which kinds of memory are your strengths and which kinds are your weaknesses. After the two of you agree on which kinds of memory are your strengths and weaknesses, list them below.

6. Your memory strengths:

7. Your memory weaknesses:

Now look at the figure titled "My Memory Strengths and Weaknesses." Color your strengths in green and your weaknesses in red.

My Memory Strengths and Weaknesses

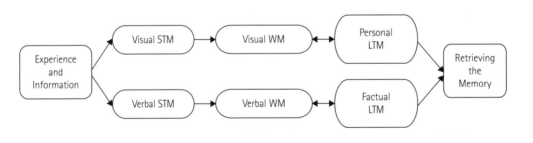

5 Memory Beliefs

Name _____ Grade _____ Date _____

Directions

Here are some statements about memory. Check the box in front of those that you believe.

❏ A person will remember something better just because he or she wants to remember it.

❏ All memories last forever.

❏ People have no control over their memory.

❏ If you can remember something five minutes later, you will almost certainly remember it tomorrow.

❏ Repeating something over and over is the best way to create a lasting memory.

❏ People can easily tell whether they have learned something well enough to remember it later.

❏ Material that is hard to memorize will be remembered better.

❏ The ability to remember things cannot be improved.

❏ Only dumb people have memory problems.

❏ A good memory technique will help you memorize anything you want to remember.

❏ If you can't remember something when someone asks you a question, it means that the information has been permanently erased from your memory.

❏ How you study has nothing to do with how well you will remember the material.

❏ If two people experience the same event, they will have identical memories of the event.

❏ People will remember something better just because they are interested in it.

❏ You should spend the same amount of time trying to memorize easy material and difficult material.

❏ The best way to study for a test is to wait until the night before the test to study.

Now, ask your trainer which of the beliefs are true and discuss the ones you marked.

6 Memorization Methods

Name _____ Grade _____ Date _____

Practice Round 1

Below is a list of 10 Spanish words. Imagine that you have to memorize their English meanings for a quiz tomorrow. Demonstrate for your trainer how you will memorize them. Your trainer will provide any materials you might need.

Vaca = Cow   Ballena = Whale

Niña = Girl   Calle = Street

Perro = Dog   Sol = Sun

Lodo = Mud   Primo = Cousin

Rojo = Red   Cerdo = Pig

With your trainer's help, write a description of the method you were using to memorize the vocabulary words.

Practice Round 2

Below is a short science lesson. Imagine that you have to memorize the facts for a test. Demonstrate for your trainer how you will learn and memorize the science facts. Your trainer will provide any materials you might need.

The heart is an organ that pumps blood through the circulatory system. The heart is divided into four chambers: two upper and two lower. The two upper chambers are called atria, with each one being called an atrium. The lower chambers consist of two ventricles. On each side of the heart, there is one atrium and one ventricle.

The thick wall that divides the two sides of the heart is called the septum. To trace the flow of blood through the heart, begin with the right atrium, where blood enters as it returns from the body. From the right atrium, the blood is pumped into the right ventricle. From there, it is pumped into a large artery that takes it to the lungs where it releases carbon dioxide and picks up oxygen. Upon returning to the lungs, the blood enters the left atrium and is pumped into the left ventricle. From the left ventricle blood is pumped out through a large artery called the aorta. Through branching arteries and capillaries it reaches all cells in the body (except those in the lungs) before once again returning to the heart.

With your trainer's help, write a description of the method you were using to memorize the science facts.

Questions

1. Tell your trainer about any other methods you use when you are trying to memorize facts and information. After discussing the methods with your trainer, decide how to describe each of them in a few words, and write the descriptions here.

2. Which of the above methods is your favorite?

3. If you want to remember something for a long time, which of your memorization methods work best?

4. Do you use different methods for different situations or different kinds of material? Explain.

5. How do you know when you have studied something long enough that you will remember it?

Memory Strategies Survey

Name _____ Grade _____ Date _____

Below is a list of different methods that students use to memorize information and remember things. Circle the word that best describes how often you use each method.

1. Repeating the information several times

   Never   Sometimes   Always

2. Making a list of things to do

   Never   Sometimes   Always

3. Writing information down several times

   Never   Sometimes   Always

4. Thinking about what I already know—
   for example, when I learn about a new
   type of wild cat, I think about what I
   already know about cats

   Never   Sometimes   Always

5. Putting words to remember in a sentence
   or story

   Never   Sometimes   Always

6. Grouping words into categories

   Never   Sometimes   Always

7. Using first-letter acronyms, such as
   HOMES for the names of the Great Lakes

   Never   Sometimes   Always

8. Using first letters in a sentence, such as
   "**E**very **G**ood **B**oy **D**oes **F**ine" to
   remember EGBDF

   Never   Sometimes   Always

9. Creating pictures or images in my head,
   such as picturing an apple when I need
   to remember the word "apple"

   Never   Sometimes   Always

10. Testing myself with flash cards   *Never*   *Sometimes*   *Always*

11. Making my own review sheet to study
    from   *Never*   *Sometimes*   *Always*

12. Reviewing or studying the same material
    every day for several days   *Never*   *Sometimes*   *Always*

13. Saying the names of objects I need to
    remember, such as saying "ball" to
    myself when I want to remember that
    I saw a ball   *Never*   *Sometimes*   *Always*

14. Placing objects or notes in a special
    location   *Never*   *Sometimes*   *Always*

15. Using another memory method a teacher
    taught me or I discovered on my own   *Never*   *Sometimes*   *Always*

8 Goals for Improving Memory

Name _____ Grade _____ Date _____

Review Lesson 4, where you colored in your memory strengths and weaknesses. List your memory weaknesses here.

In school, what do you have the most difficulty remembering?

At home, what kinds of things do you frequently forget?

With your trainer's help, decide on the three most important goals that you have for improving your memory and write them here.

1.

2.

3.

Explain why each goal is important to you.

1.

2.

3.

Explain how you will know when you have achieved each goal.

1.

2.

3.

By what date would you like to achieve each goal?

1.

2.

3.

Your trainer will write three goals that he or she has for your memory improvement here.

1.

2.

3.

Which of the trainer's goals do you agree with?

Is there anything else you would like to gain from memory training? If yes, explain.

9 A Memory Experiment

Name _____ Grade _____ Date _____

A Memory Experiment: Part I

When your trainer says "begin," you will have one minute to memorize the list of words below. You must memorize them without copying them onto paper.

Shirt	Shoes
Tomato	Cabbage
Couch	Pliers
Hammer	Dresser
Carrots	Beans
Gloves	Pajamas
Wrench	Bed
Table	Screwdriver

Things That Can Harm Memory

Here are some things that can harm the brain's memory center:

➤ Stress and anxiety
➤ Depression
➤ A concussion or head injury
➤ Loss of oxygen
➤ Problems controlling diabetes
➤ A very high fever
➤ Drug abuse
➤ Getting very little sleep

A Memory Experiment: Part I Continued

A few minutes ago you tried to memorize a list of 16 words. Write the words you remember below.

A Memory Experiment: Part II

When your trainer says "begin" you will have one minute to memorize the new list of words below. This time the words are grouped by categories. First, focus on the name of each category. Then review the words in each category. You must memorize the words without copying them on paper.

Sports	Animals	Buildings	Colors
Baseball	Fox	Church	Brown
Soccer	Moose	Barn	Violet
Football	Turtle	Garage	Orange
Hockey	Elephant	Store	Green

Things That Can Help Memory

Here are some things that help memory work better. Check the ones that you do.

❏ Organizing the information you want to remember

❏ Repeating things to yourself

❏ Studying material more than once

❏ Practicing a skill many times

❏ Testing yourself or having someone test you

❏ Making yourself remember, instead of just looking at the answer

❏ Thinking about the information you are studying

❏ Taking breaks when you study

❏ Getting plenty of sleep

❏ Creating pictures of words in your mind

❏ Naming things that you see

A Memory Experiment: Part II, Continued

A few minutes ago you tried to memorize a list of 16 words grouped by category. Write the individual words (but not the category names) below.

Now tally the number correct from Part I and Part II of the memory experiment and compute the percentage correct. Did you do better on Part II than on Part I? Is so, why do you think this happened?

Assignment

Organizing and grouping words or factual information by categories can help you remember it. For example, grouping shopping items by category would help you remember the items. This coming week, try grouping science or social studies facts when you study them. Bring your grouped sheet of facts to show your trainer next week.

10 Review and Reflections

Name _____ Grade _____ Date _____

List some new things that you have learned about how everybody's memory works.

List some new things that you have learned about how your memory works.

Describe a memory failure you have had within the past week.

Describe a memory success you have had within the past week.

Do you now believe that you can influence how well your memory works?

How important is it for you to improve your memory?

Since beginning this training, have you tried any new method for improving your memory? If so, what is it?

What do you think and feel about these memory training sessions?

11 Repetition

Name _____ Grade _____ Date _____

Review of the Memory Experiment

Tell your trainer about any times you've tried grouping words or facts by category since the Memory Experiment session. If you have a grouped list, show it to your trainer. Grouping items by category works for two reasons. First, we remember words, items, or facts better when they are stored together. Second, if we can't immediately retrieve the information we want, we can start thinking of things in that category and often we will then "recognize" what we were trying to remember.

Practice Round 1

Below is a list of words that cannot be grouped by category. Read each word aloud once. After you have read the list, cover it up and immediately write down as many words as you can remember in the right-hand column.

<u>Write the words here</u>

Knees
Sprout
Antler
Trust
Heavy
Polish
Skill
Bottom
Apron
Stack

Repetition

Repetition (repeating things over and over) is a basic method that most people use when they want to remember something for more than a few seconds. Repetition allows you to maintain information in short-term memory for a longer time period. When information remains in short-term memory longer, you have a better chance of encoding it into long-term memory. In everyday life, you use repetition to remember something that is not written down. For example, you might repeat a phone number several times after someone tells you the number. Or you might repeat a list of chores a parent tells you to do. Although it helps short-term memory, simple repetition is not the best memorization method for long-term memory.

There are different ways of repeating information to yourself. When repeating a list of words, it is best to repeat the whole list of words together, rather than just repeating one word at a time. For example, if the words to memorize are "empire, colony, and republic," you should NOT say "empire" several times before saying the other words. Instead, you would repeat all three words together several times. Also, repetition usually works better when you whisper the words to yourself.

Practice Round 2

Your trainer will now slowly read you a list of 10 words to remember. When you hear the first word, keep whispering it until you hear the second word, then add the second word, and then keep adding each new word to the list as you hear it. For example, if the words are "apple, lettuce, plates," keep repeating "apple" until you hear "lettuce," and then say "apple, lettuce" until you hear "plates," and then keep saying "apple, lettuce, plates." Now, practice three other words with your trainer.

Now use this method as your trainer reads the 10 words. Whisper the words loud enough for your trainer to hear. Afterward, write the words you remember here.

Did you remember more words in Practice Round 2 than in Round 1? If so, why do you think this happened?

Kim's Story, Continued

Kim, who was then in eighth grade, used the same method of memorization that she had been using since second grade. When she had to memorize something, she would copy it over and over again, writing the fact 10 times in a row on a sheet of paper. This was a very time-consuming process. The next time she studied, she would read and repeat the fact over and over. After copying and reviewing the facts, Kim almost always thought she knew them, but when she took the test, she could not remember very many of the facts.

Kim was frustrated and worried. She was beginning to think she was just dumb. She thought her methods were good memorization methods. They had worked pretty well when she was in early elementary. She didn't realize that most of her classmates were no longer using these basic repetition methods. They had moved on to other memorization strategies that not only worked well but saved a lot of time.

Luckily, Kim's tutor offered to teach Kim some better memory strategies. Kim was curious. She accepted the offer.

LESSON 12 Repeating Written Information

This lesson is optional for upper level students. Go to the lower level lesson if you would like to complete it.

LESSON 13 Using Repetition to Study Spelling

This lesson is optional for upper level students. Go to the lower level lesson if you would like to complete it.

LESSON 14 Chunking

This lesson is required for upper level students. Use the lower level lesson because it is identical to the upper level lesson.

LESSON 15 Review of Repetition and Chunking

This lesson is optional for upper level students. Go to the lower level lesson if you would like to complete it.

LESSON 16 Using Chunking to Memorize Spelling

This lesson is recommended for upper level students, especially those who have weekly spelling tests. Go to the lower level lesson to complete it.

17 Putting Words Into Sentences and Stories

Name _____ Grade _____ Date _____

Repetition and Chunking Practice

Combine repetition and chunking as you memorize the list of words below. Keep going over them until you think you will be able to remember all of them. Then cover them up and say them.

Coffee	Kitchen	Sweater	Cabbage	Umbrella	Spider
Violin	Basket	Saddle	Bucket	Thief	Patch

Putting Words in Sentences

Another way to remember words is to put them into sentences. For example, "bananas" is easier to remember when it is in the sentence "Monkeys love bananas."

Practice

For each word below, create a sentence that includes the word. The sentences should stand alone; they should not create a story. The sentences will be easier to remember if they are funny or are easy to picture in your mind. Imagine that you have to memorize the names of the states below because they have something in common.

<u>Write the sentences you create here</u>

Washington

Virginia

Florida

Missouri

Indiana

Rhode Island

Now, try to remember the sentences you wrote. Then "pull out" the words you need to remember and write them here.

Putting the Words Into a Story

Another way to remember words is to put all of them into one story. When you recall the story, you will recognize the words you want to remember.

Practice

Make up a short story using the words below. First, think of what the story is going to be about, and tell your trainer the idea of your story. Then write the story and include each of the words. Try to make the story funny and it will be easier to remember.

Storm	Airplane	Tomatoes	Rope
Pancakes	Wheels	Gloves	Mountain

Write the story here. Each sentence should have at least one of the words in it.

Now cover up the words and the story. Retell the story aloud, and as you come to each word on the list, write it here.

Assignment

Try using the story method with words or facts you need to remember for a science or social studies chapter. To judge the effectiveness of this method, first study a chapter subsection like you normally do. Then study the next subsection by creating a story. You can try this now or during a later session.

18 Comparing Memory Methods

Name _____ Grade _____ Date _____

During the last session, you memorized a list of 12 words, using the repetition and chunking methods combined. Write the words you remember here.

During the last session, you created six sentences to help you remember six states. Try to remember those sentences now and write the names of the states here.

During the last session, you also made up a story to help remember eight words. Try to remember the story now and write the words here.

Compute the percentage correct for each set of words. With which method did you remember the most?

Last time, you also might have studied from a textbook using your usual method first and then putting key words and facts into a story. If so, your trainer will now ask you some questions on each section.

Compute the percentage correct for each subsection. With which method did you remember the most?

Why do you think putting words and facts into sentences or a story might help you remember them better than simple repetition? Write in your answer.

The answer to the above question is that people remember better when they do more with the information than simply repeating it. This is called *processing the information more deeply*. For example, thinking about the information or using the information in a story is processing it more deeply.

19 Using Arithmetic to Build Memory

Name _____ Grade _____ Date _____

Arithmetic Exercise to Build Memory

Working memory and long-term memory help you do mathematics problems. It works the other way too; practicing arithmetic facts can help make your working memory stronger. Here's how it works. Your trainer will show you two arithmetic flash cards. Tell her or him the answer to each card, while trying to remember the answers you gave in order. For example, when you see $5 + 2$, say "7" and when you see $4 + 5$, say "9." Then, when the last card is put down, say "7, 9." When this becomes easy to do, you will practice remembering three answers in a row, then four, and so on. Now try remembering two in row with some arithmetic flash cards. See if you can remember 10 pairs of answers without making any mistakes.

How did you do? If you remembered the correct sequence for all 10 pairs, now try to remember 10 correct sequences of three answers.

Do you have a strategy for remembering the sequence of answers? If yes, explain your strategy to your trainer. If no, think of a strategy now and try using it.

Assignment

If you have arithmetic flash cards at home you might ask a parent to do this exercise with you. Always use a set of flash cards for which you already know the answers. The arithmetic should be easy, only remembering the answers in order should be hard. Your trainer will send home directions for your parent.

Working Memory Overload in the Classroom

Look back at the information on working memory in Lesson 3. Then, explain to your trainer what working memory is. Also, recall which half of your working memory is stronger: visual or verbal (see the figure in Lesson 4 if you are not sure).

The typical classroom is a busy place where most students have a hard time keeping track of everything they are supposed to be doing and remembering. When this happens to you, it is probably because your working memory is overloaded. When your working memory is overloaded, you will either forget some information you need right now or you will not be able to complete what you were doing. Signs of an overloaded working memory are listed below. Check the ones that you have experienced.

❏ Forgetting some of the directions ❏ Forgetting what you were going to say
❏ Losing your place ❏ Asking for something to be repeated
❏ Difficulty completing math problems ❏ Difficulty taking notes
❏ Difficulty understanding what you read ❏ Difficulty writing down your ideas

Now, tell your trainer about a time when your working memory was overloaded and you either forgot something or couldn't keep up with what you needed to do.

20 Using Cards to Build Memory

Name _____ Grade _____ Date _____

A deck of regular playing cards can also be used to strengthen your working memory. To play, you must remember cards you have seen a certain number of cards back. For example, it works like this when you are asked to remember what you saw two cards back: if you see 6—3—4—7—5 one at a time, you would say "six" when the 4 is shown, "three" when the 7 is shown, and "four" when the 5 is shown.

Let's start by having you remember the card you saw just before the current card. You will get to look at each card for two seconds. Say the name of the card you are supposed to remember as soon as another card is flipped over. When you make your first mistake, you must start over with a new set of cards. When you can correctly recall 10 cards in a row, you can go to the next level, where you will need to remember what you saw two cards before. Your trainer will keep adding another card to remember farther back until you hit your level of difficulty.

Try the game now with your trainer and see how far you can advance.

A Strategy for the Card Game

Explain to your trainer what you were doing to remember the cards.

As you try to remember cards farther and farther back in the sequence, the game will become harder. To succeed, you must develop a strategy. Simply looking at the cards and automatically remembering them will no longer work. Here is a beginning strategy for remembering what you saw three cards before, with the cards 5, 3, Jack, 3, 9, and 7 as an example: When you see the 5, keep quietly saying to yourself "five, five, five" until the 3 is flipped up; then say "five, three" as many times as you can until the Jack is flipped up; and then "five, three, Jack" until the 3 is flipped up. Then, after you say "five" aloud, quickly say to yourself "three, Jack, three" until the 9 is flipped up, and so on. This makes the cards easier to remember because you are verbalizing what you see and because you are using repetition. Try the strategy now, if you were not already doing it.

Practice and Keep It Challenging

It's not easy to actually make your working memory stronger. It is similar to making your muscles stronger. That is, you must exercise frequently and push the limits of what you are capable of doing. For example, walking will not make you a stronger runner. With working memory, occasionally playing a memory game will do nothing to make it stronger. This is why you should do one of the working memory exercises a few times each week. Also, whenever you master one level, move up to the next level to keep it challenging.

Assignment

Ask a parent or friend to play this memory-building game with you. Your trainer will give you a sheet of directions that you can take home.

21 Remembering Locations to Build Memory

Name _____ Grade _____ Date _____

Trying to remember what you saw and where you saw it can make your working memory stronger. In the tables below you will see Xs and Os in certain locations. Try to remember where they are. When your trainer covers up a table, mark the Xs and Os in the correct places in the table on the right.

<u>Fill in Xs and Os here</u>

		O
X		
	X	

	O	
X		X
		O

	O		
	X		
		O	X
X			O

			O	
O		X		
				X
	X	O		O
			X	

22 Picturing Verbal Information

Name _____ Grade _____ Date _____

Practice Round 1

When your trainer says "begin," you will have one minute to memorize the list of words below. Try to memorize them by reading through the list as many times as you can. When time expires, cover up the list.

Castle	Table	Spider	Pants	Skateboard	Gloves
Potato	Fireplace	Banana	Rainbow	Tennis	Camel

Suggestions for Supporting Your Working Memory in the Classroom

In the classroom, your working memory can easily become overloaded. When this happens, your ability to complete work, learn, and remember is reduced. Your teacher might do things to reduce the load on your working memory, but you can also make things more manageable for your working memory. Listed below are some things you can do. Check the ones you already do, and discuss these with your trainer.

❑ Keep my desk and backpack neat and organized

❑ Have the materials I need before class begins

❑ Repeat directions to myself right after the teacher says them

❑ Repeat directions to myself until I am able to write them down

❑ Organize information before I try to study it

❑ Do an assignment, activity, or project one step at a time

❑ Try to picture the information I am reading or hearing

Assignment

From the list above, select one classroom suggestion that you are not doing and try it this coming week. Next week, tell your trainer what you did and whether you think it helped your learning.

Practice Round 1 Continued

A few minutes ago, you tried to memorize a list of 12 words. Write the words you remember here.

Visualizing and Imagery

Our brains store verbal memories of what we hear and read, and they store visual memories of what we see or picture in our minds. Picturing verbal information in our minds is called visualizing or imagery. When we visualize, the memories we create are just as strong as the memories of things we have actually seen. It is important to put information we want to learn into both our visual and verbal memory systems. Most of what we must learn in school is verbal information. Sometimes, we automatically visualize the verbal information, such as when we are reading a story. However, most of the time verbal information will not become stored in our visual memory unless we deliberately visualize it. If we visualize the verbal information, we will have another way of remembering it when we cannot remember it verbally. That's why most students remember words better when they visualize them instead of just repeating them. So, when trying to memorize verbal information, visualizing or creating images will make it easier for you to remember.

Practice Round 2

Below is another list of words to memorize. After you read each word, close your eyes for a few seconds and picture the item in your mind. When you have finished going through the list, tell your trainer and cover up the list.

| Baseball | Hammer | Airplane | Carrot | Turkey | Doctor |
| Saddle | Mouse | Flower | Robber | Telephone | Beaver |

Suggestions for Supporting Your Working Memory During Home Study

Here are some things you can do at home to keep things manageable for your working memory. Check the ones that you already do and discuss these with your trainer.

❏ Have a desk or study area that I always use when I study

❏ Have all the materials I need, such as paper and a dictionary, in my study area

❏ Study in a quiet place where I can't hear music, a television, or conversations

❏ When doing an assignment, such as a math assignment, keep an example of how to complete the problems in front of me

❏ When doing assignments in which I have to keep track of several things, keep a list of those things in front of me; for example, when editing and revising a writing assignment, keep a list of all the kinds of errors I should check for

❏ Don't try to do other things while I study; work on only one assignment at a time, and complete each part of an assignment before going on to the next part

❏ Before starting a writing assignment I make an outline of my ideas

❏ Read difficult or confusing information at least twice

❏ Take breaks when it becomes difficult to concentrate

Assignment

Select one home suggestion that you are not doing and try it this coming week. Next week, tell your trainer what you did and whether you think it helped your learning.

Practice Round 2 Continued

A few minutes ago, you visualized a list of 12 words. Write the words you remember here.

Now count the number correct from Practice Rounds 1 and 2. On which Round did you do better?

Why do you think you did better on this Round? Did visualizing make a difference? Discuss this with your trainer.

Visualizing Directions

Visualizing multistep directions can help you remember them better. Imagining yourself doing each step of the directions you hear or read will make them even more memorable. As your trainer reads each step, visualize what needs to be done and imagine yourself doing it.

Now describe your images for your trainer. Were you in the scenes?

Now say all the steps in order. Do you think visualizing helped?

Making Images Memorable

Imagery can be used to remember many different types of information, and there are specific imagery methods that you will learn in later lessons. For now, it's important to realize that you will remember images best when the images you create are focused on the specific information, contain some kind of action, and are funny.

Assignment

This coming week, make a special effort to do more visualizing of verbal information that you need to remember. Examples include visualizing directions and visualizing new facts that you need to learn.

23 Naming and Describing What You See

Name _____ Grade _____ Date _____

Practice Round 1

You will have 15 seconds to look at the shapes below.

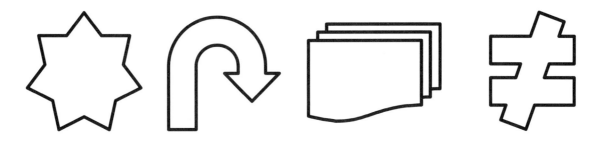

Now draw the shapes from memory on a blank sheet of paper.

How did you do? Did you try to remember any of them by describing the shape to yourself? For example, you might have said "A star with seven points" for the first shape.

Verbalizing Visual Information

Naming and describing what we see strengthens memories for visual information, because that process encodes the information into both our verbal and visual memory systems. Sometimes, the objects are difficult to name or describe, such as the middle object above, but usually we can use words to describe what we see. Verbalizing works for any kind of visual information, not just for objects. For example, if you wish to remember who was in a scene, you could name or describe the individuals. Also, you could use words to describe the location or movement of something.

Practice Round 2

As you look at the shapes below, use words to describe them to yourself. Say your descriptions aloud so that your trainer can hear you.

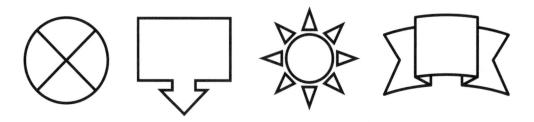

Now draw the shapes from memory on a blank sheet of paper.

Did you remember the details better this time?

Practice Round 3

On a blank sheet of paper, draw a simple map that illustrates how to get from your school to your home. Now show the map to your trainer and give verbal directions as you point to locations on the map.

Dual Encoding

By drawing the map and giving verbal directions, you helped your trainer to encode the directions both visually and verbally. Encoding it both ways is called dual encoding. You were also doing dual encoding when you practiced visualizing verbal information in the previous lesson. Whenever we use dual encoding, we have a better chance of remembering. Dual encoding seldom happens automatically. We usually have to make a special, conscious effort to do it.

Assignment

This coming week, make a special effort to use dual encoding in at least two situations where you really need to remember something. One of the situations should involve the verbalizing of visual information. Be prepared to tell your trainer about your dual encoding experiences the next time you meet for a lesson.

24 Grouping Words by Category

Name _____ Grade _____ Date _____

Our verbal memory system has a natural tendency to organize information. Things that logically go together are closely linked in our verbal memory storage. For example, scientists have proven that the names of mammals are more closely linked to each other in the brain than they are linked with other kinds of animals. A well-organized memory storage system has "files" of information that belong together. Your trainer will now ask you some questions to illustrate how related facts are closely linked in your memory.

We can make our memories stronger by making sure new information is encoded into the files where it belongs. In the Memory Experiment lesson, you learned that words grouped by categories were much easier to remember than ungrouped words. Organizing and categorizing information is a very effective memorization method.

Practice Round 1

On a blank sheet of paper, organize the words below into categories. Then memorize the names of the categories, the number of items under each category, and finally the names of the individual items under each category. When you are finished memorizing, cover the words.

Division	Dictator
Newspaper	Telephone
Mountain	Average
Mayor	Lake
Radio	Internet
Island	President
Fractions	Letter
King	Desert
Equation	

Now, write as many words as you can remember below. You don't need to write the name of the categories, but try to recall the words by category, not randomly. When you can't remember all of the items, try running through that category in your mind and you might "recognize" the missing items.

How did you do? Do you think organized information is easier to remember?

Practice Round 2

Imagine you need to memorize the social studies facts below for a quiz. The social studies unit is about the Aztecs of ancient Mexico. On a sheet of paper, logically organize the facts so that you will remember them better.

➤ They created fine stone carvings.
➤ Their capital was on the island of Texcoco.
➤ The priests held tremendous power.
➤ They developed a precise calendar.
➤ They had a great temple in the middle of their city.
➤ The rich wore fine cotton cloaks.
➤ Human sacrifices to the gods were common.
➤ The farmer's market was on the north side of the city.
➤ The sun god was their highest ranking god.

Other Ways of Organizing Information to Make It Memorable

Putting items into categories is not the only way to organize information so that it is memorable. Other ways of organizing information include:

➢ Alphabetizing
➢ Filing by topic
➢ Putting things in order from first to last
➢ Comparing and contrasting
➢ Sorting into known versus unknown facts
➢ Using headings and subheadings to identify topics in your notes

Reorganizing Information

Teacher's notes and textbooks are usually organized pretty well. However, not everyone's memory filing system is the same. You may find some information easier to remember if you reorganize it in ways that make sense to you.

Assignment

With your trainer, discuss classes where you have to memorize lots of information for tests. Talk about how you might group, organize, or reorganize information to make it more memorable. Agree on what material you will try this method with, do it during the coming week, and bring in what you did to show your trainer.

25 # Imagining Yourself in the Scene

Name _____ Grade _____ Date _____

Another way to use imagery to make factual information more memorable is to imagine yourself in the scene that you are reading about. For example, when reading literature or history, place yourself right in the scene. You should feel like you are actually there, getting a close-up view of what's happening. Although it's not necessary, you may even move about and interact with the objects or characters who are there. When you do this, your personal memory system will become connected with the factual information, making it easier to remember.

Practice

Read the selection below about the American Revolutionary Army spending the winter at Valley Forge. As you read the information, stop now and then and imagine yourself being there and seeing everything that is happening from up close. Imagine as many details as possible, and think about how you would sense it, such as how cold you might feel. Also, think about the thoughts and feelings you would have if you were one of the soldiers. Continue doing this for a few minutes.

> In the winter of 1777, George Washington took his 12,000 troops to Valley Forge, Pennsylvania. The valley had a creek running through it, and it was surrounded by mountains. The soldiers were strong and healthy when they arrived. They quickly gathered logs from the surrounding woods and constructed cabins to protect them from winter weather. Their clothes were so raggedy they had a hard time staying warm. The men had to endure not just the cold, but wet and damp conditions. There were also shortages of food and many of the men were near starvation at times. Occasionally, some potatoes and meat would be brought to the valley camp, but there was never enough to feed everyone well. Even the army's horses suffered; hundreds of them died from starvation over the winter. However, diseases such as pneumonia and influenza were the main killers. The conditions in the camp allowed diseases to spread, and there were few doctors and almost no medicines. Most of the men were ill at one time or another during the harsh winter, and 2,000 of them would die from disease before summer. Family members of the soldiers came to Valley Forge to help out as much as they could.

Some women even lost their lives trying to gather supplies for the soldiers. It was difficult for the army to maintain its strength and a positive attitude, but George Washington and his loyal troops did not give up despite their misery. When summer came they emerged from this Pennsylvania valley to continue their fight with the British army.

Now tell your trainer what you saw and felt as you imagined yourself at Valley Forge with the revolutionary army.

Assignment

Try this technique the next time you read social studies material. When you take the test on the material, try to remember yourself in the scene and what you saw and felt before you start answering the test questions.

26 Using Locations to Remember Information

Name _____ Grade _____ Date _____

The memory strategy you are about to learn has been used since the days of the ancient Greeks. This strategy, which is called *loci*, involves the use of imagery. In the images, you link or associate items to be remembered with rooms or objects in your home.

First, identify the rooms in your home. List them (at least eight) here.

Second, identify the objects in your bedroom. List them (at least eight), in the order they appear when you open the door and go around the room to your left.

Practice Round 1

Imagine that the products listed below are exported from an African nation. Let's say that you need to memorize these for a social studies quiz. For each item, create an image linking that item with one of the rooms in your home. Use each room only once. The image will be more memorable if it is funny. As you create each image, share it with your trainer.

Cattle   Oil   Diamonds   Cotton   Lumber   Gold   Snakes   Cement

Practice Round 2

Imagine the list below names immigrants in the order they settled in the Boston area. Let's say you need to memorize them in order. Go around the objects in your room in order as you create a link with each group. The image will be more memorable if it contains some action. As you create each image, share it with your trainer.

Indians   Vikings   Pilgrims   Irish   Chinese   Italians   Russians

Why Loci Works

Loci works because you are linking a word or fact with something you already know and won't forget, such as the rooms in your house. When you recall the rooms and objects, the images you created will automatically be recalled. When you see what's in the image, you will recognize the information you want to remember.

Assignment

Try using loci the next time you need to memorize some social studies or science facts.

27 Pegword

Name _____ Grade _____ Date _____

Review

During the last lesson you memorized a list of exports, using the loci method to associate each one with a room in your home. Now, mentally go through your home and picture each room. When you do, the item you placed in each room should appear and you will recognize it as one of the answers. Write the items you can recall here.

Now, do the same for the list of immigrants you memorized by associating them with objects in your bedroom. To keep the immigrants in order, go through your bedroom objects in order. Write the sequence here.

How well did loci work for you?

Pegword

The pegword method is similar to loci. With pegword, you also use imagery to link items to be remembered with other things that are well established in your memory. Pegword also can be used to keep items in order if that is required.

First, use repetition to memorize the numbers and their pegwords below. You already know how to count. For now, you just need to associate a pegword and a number. If you have trouble remembering the pegword, think of words that rhyme with the number. Do not visualize the numbers with the pegwords; keep the encoding verbal at this point.

After reviewing the list, cover it up and recite it three times for your trainer. If necessary, copy the list a couple times.

One is a bun

Two is a shoe

Three is a tree

Four is a door

Five is a hive (beehive)

Six is sticks

Seven is heaven

Eight is a gate

Nine is a vine

Ten is a hen

Practice Round 1

When using pegword, start with "bun" and use the pegwords in order. Create an image that links, or pairs, each pegword with the item to be remembered. For example, if the first item on your list is carrots, you might picture a bunch of carrots sticking out of bun. Now, use pegword to memorize the shopping list below. Share each image with your trainer as you create it.

Knife   Flower   Toothbrush   Peanuts   Napkins   Ketchup   Bread   Sweater

Practice Round 2

Most people are able to link more than one set of items to the same pegwords without the images and lists getting confused. So, try memorizing another list with the same pegwords. The list below consists of some different types of cancer. They are in order, with the first one on the list being the most deadly. Let's say you need to remember them in order for a science quiz. This time, you don't have to share your images with your trainer. Ask your trainer about any words you don't know.

Lung   Colon   Breast   Leukemia (Blood)   Bladder   Stomach   Kidney   Skin

Have a discussion with your trainer about other types of information or situations for which pegword would be a good strategy to use.

Kim's Story Continued

Kim got into the routine of the memory training sessions and after a while she actually enjoyed coming. Some of the methods really fit her personality. She was very talkative and enjoyed stories, so putting words into stories she created was fun and easy, and later she had no problem remembering the stories. Kim also had a good imagination and a good sense of humor. As a result, strategies like pegword, where she could create funny images, were right up her alley. The interesting thing was that Kim had always had difficulty remembering details when someone showed her a picture. Yet, when she created images in her head, she could easily remember them and the information linked to them.

When Kim came in for memory lessons, the trainer would quiz her about information she had tried to memorize in previous sessions. Kim almost always remembered more when she studied the material with one of the new strategies she had learned. Sometimes her improved memory was so convincing that Kim didn't even need to be told to practice it or start using it. For example, Kim was so impressed with putting words into categories that she started using the method right away.

One of Kim's most difficult classes was Language Arts. She seldom did well on the literature quizzes, especially when she had to remember details from a book. After reading the selection as she normally did, Kim reread it, and this time she stopped and imagined herself in the scenes, closely watching the characters. The next day when the quiz was handed out, Kim was really nervous. She answered almost all the questions, but wasn't sure (she seldom was) if they were right. When she got her score the next day, it was one of the best scores on a literature quiz she had ever had.

LESSON 28   Review and Reflections

Name ————————————————— Grade ——— Date ————

Review of the Last Lesson

First, recite the list of pegwords, beginning with "One is a bun." Now use pegword to recall the shopping list of eight items. First, think of "bun," and you should see the first item pictured with it. Continue through the pegwords and write the shopping list here.

Now use the same method to recall the different types of cancer in order of deadliness, and write them here.

Review and Reflection Questions

1. How are you feeling about the memory training at this point?

2. Which memory exercise or strategy do you like the most?

3. Which memory exercise or strategy is hard to do?

4. Which memory exercises or strategies have you tried using at school or home?

5. Have you been more successful at remembering things? If yes, give some examples.

6. What kinds of things are you still forgetting that you wish you could remember better?

29 Using Study Cards

Name _____ Grade _____ Date _____

Nearly every student uses study cards or "flash cards" at one time or another. A question or term is written on one side, and the answer or definition is written on the other side. Study cards have several advantages; for example, they can easily be used by other people to test you. If used correctly, they can be very effective.

Practice Round 1

Use index cards to create study cards for the following vocabulary terms.

Ombudsman = mediator	Lesion = wound
Elide = ignore	Clabber = thick, sour milk
Trawl = large fishing net	Quest = a search
Pugilism = sport of boxing	Obdurate = stubborn
Imminent = about to happen	Desiccate = dry out
Blarney = flattering speech	Thespian = actor

Now explain to your trainer all the ways you would use these study cards to memorize.

Practice Round 2

One of the most effective ways to use study cards is to sort them into piles each time you review them. Follow the steps below with the vocabulary cards you just created.

1. As you go through them the first time, put the ones you instantly know the answers to in the "know" pile. Put the others in the "don't know" pile.
2. Keep going through the "don't know" cards. When you are confident that you now know the answer to a card, add that card to the "know" pile.
3. When all the cards have been placed in the "know" pile, mix them up and review them one more time.

More Tips for Using Study Cards

1. When studying alone, always test yourself. That is, do not look at the answer until you've given one. If it's difficult to remember, take time and make an effort to

actually retrieve the answer. Guess if you have to. Then check to see if your answer is correct.

2. Don't always study the cards in the same order. Mix them up. If you don't, the cards in the middle will not get remembered as well.

3. When studying alone, say aloud or whisper the questions and answers to yourself.

4. Use the visualizing method whenever the information can be pictured.

5. If it's vocabulary, you can also use the keyword method (see Lesson 40).

6. Spread out your reviews of the cards. Reviewing too often is not helpful (see Lesson 43).

7. Have someone test you with the cards.

8. Always follow the sorting procedures described in Practice Round 2.

Assignment

If you are using study cards for a class, bring them to a future memory lesson. Also, bring your social studies book to the next memory lesson.

30 Thinking About the Information

Name _____ Grade _____ Date _____

Review

Explain to your trainer how to use study cards if you really want to efficiently learn and remember the material on the cards. Think of the tips at the end of the last lesson.

Practice Round 1

Below are six social studies facts that are probably new to you. Study them for a few minutes as you normally would, without writing down any of the information.

➤ Although Puerto Rico is not a U.S. state, the people of Puerto Rico are U.S. citizens.

➤ In Greece, which includes 2,000 islands, many people depend on the sea for their living.

➤ The Romans built 50,000 miles of roads made out of stone and gravel.

➤ When kings used to say that they ruled by "divine right," it meant that their powers and right to rule came from God.

➤ In democracies that do not have a president, a "prime minister" is the highest elected official.

➤ The Mekong River begins in the mountains of Tibet and flows into the China Sea when it reaches Vietnam.

Elaboration

Thinking about the information you are trying to learn is another strategy that makes the information more memorable. Thinking about the information is especially effective when you think about how the new facts are connected with related facts that you already know. This kind of thinking is called *elaboration*. For example, when you read some new information about George Washington's life, stopping to think about what you already know about Washington is elaboration. Elaboration works because it "opens up" your memory file on the subject. Once the memory file is open, the new, related information will be stored in the correct file. Elaboration improves the understanding, storage, and retrieval of the new information. Elaboration is such a powerful technique that it is one of the "big three" long-term memory strategies, along with organization and visualization.

Your teachers often elaborate for you by directly stating some connections between old information and new information. Your teachers may also encourage your elaborative thinking by giving you examples. However, elaboration is even more effective when you do it yourself. There are a few ways to do it. Here are the options:

1. When you hear or read a new fact or some new information, pause to think about it and try to remember what you already know about the subject.

2. If you believe you know nothing about the new topic, think about similar information. For example, you might not know anything about the African country of Uganda, but you do know some things about Africa. So pause and think about what you already know about Africa.

3. Compare and contrast the new fact with related facts you know, especially thinking about similarities and differences. Perhaps you have read that humans and chimpanzees may share a common ancestor. Thinking about the similarities and differences between humans and chimpanzees would make this new information more memorable.

4. Try to make sense out of the new information. For example, if your teacher says that global warming will cause ocean levels to rise, stop and think about how this would happen. You might conclude that global warming will melt glaciers and that this will add more water to the oceans.

5. Try to figure out *why* the new fact or information is true or makes sense. Whenever you recognize a new fact, ask yourself, "Why does this make sense?" The process of trying to answer the why question will link the new fact with related facts you already know.

Practice Round 2

Below are some social studies facts. For each fact (or the part of each fact that is new to you), stop and think about what you already know about the subject. Think aloud so your trainer can hear you and help you.

➤ King Tut's tomb contained furniture and statues of servants.
➤ Mexico City, which is surrounded by mountains, has the worst air pollution in the world.
➤ When Napoleon attacked Portugal, the Portuguese king went to Brazil, where he took over the government.
➤ The Mongols, who were great horsemen, were able to conquer so many lands that they created the largest empire the world has ever known.
➤ After a dictator ruled England for 11 years, the English parliament invited Charles, the son of the last king, to come back to England and be king.
➤ In Australia, the wide open land where almost no one lives is called the "bush."

Practice Round 3

Below are more social studies facts. For each fact, ask yourself, "Why does this make sense?" Then answer the question as best you can. Think aloud so your trainer can hear you and help you.

➤ After the invention of the printing press, universities stopped teaching memorization methods to students.

➤ Australia is the smallest continent.

➤ Portugal, a nation on the Atlantic coast just north of Africa, was the first European nation to explore the Atlantic coast of Africa.

➤ As Napoleon's army retreated from Russia in the winter of 1812, many of his men died without fighting in a battle.

➤ After the invention of the steam engine, factories were able to produce more goods.

➤ The Egyptians were the first ancient people to have a 12-month calendar with 365 days.

Practice Round 4

You can use elaboration when you are reading literature or studying from a textbook. To do so, you must first be looking for new facts and information as you read. Whenever you come to a new fact, ask and answer the "why" question before you go on. If the material you are reading has several new facts per paragraph, pick the fact you think is the most important and then elaborate by answering the "why" question. Try this method now with several paragraphs from your social studies or science book.

At this point, what do you think and feel about the elaboration strategy?

Assignment

Bring your social studies or science book to the next memory lesson.

31 Remembering What You Read

Name _____ Grade _____ Date _____

Review

During the last lesson, you studied three sets of social studies facts. Now recall the facts you studied without elaboration. The first fact was about Puerto Rico. Tell the facts you remember to your trainer.

Now recall the second set of facts, the ones you studied by thinking about what you already knew about the subject. The first fact was about King Tut.

Now recall the set of facts you studied by asking and answering the "why" question. The first fact was about the invention of the printing press.

Which set of facts did you remember the best?

Practice

From your social studies book or some other book, read the first selection as you normally would if you were reading it to prepare for a test. Then select four new facts from the reading and write them here.

1.

2.

3.

4.

PERSAR

There are ways of reading information that not only make it easier to understand but also make it more memorable. The PERSAR method is one of these. PERSAR stands for *Preview, Elaborate, Read, Select, Answer*, and *Review*.

Preview

Before you begin to read a selection, preview the material by:

- ❏ Reading the title
- ❏ Reading all the subtitles
- ❏ Reading all the bolded and italicized words
- ❏ Looking at the pictures, graphs, maps, and other visuals
- ❏ Reading the picture captions and the information on the visuals
- ❏ Reading any review questions at the end of the selection

Now preview the next reading selection. After you finish previewing, look at the preview list above and check the boxes of the steps you did.

Elaborate

After the preview you will know the subject of the reading. Now take a couple of minutes to think about what you already know about this topic. Now, write three things that you already know about the topic.

1.

2.

3.

Read

Now read the material a paragraph at a time, trying to visualize (picture) what you are reading about. Pause after reading each paragraph to complete the *select* and *answer* steps below. Then do the same for the remaining paragraphs until you finish the reading.

Select

After reading each paragraph, select what you think is the most important fact or piece of information in the paragraph.

Answer

Now that you have selected the most important fact, ask and answer the "Why does this fact make sense" question. For the first four paragraphs, write the most important fact and then your answer to the "why" question about that fact. For the remaining paragraphs, tell your trainer the fact and your answer.

Fact

Answer

Fact

Answer

Fact

Answer

Fact

Answer

Review

After you have finished the reading selection, look over the headings, subheadings, italicized or bolded words, and visuals again. Also, read what you wrote down during the Elaborate, Select, and Answer steps. Then answer any review questions at the end of the selection.

Why PERSAR Works

The *Preview* and *Elaborate* steps "open" your memory files on the topic. Now these files are in your working memory and are ready to accept new information. As you *Read* the material, it will now be "filed" with the correct information, instead of just being randomly put into memory. The *Select* and *Answer* steps are elaboration steps that make you process the information more "deeply," making it more memorable. Answering the "why" question also builds more connections with the correct memory files. The *Review* step further reinforces the new memory connections you have just created by making you retrieve the new information for the first time.

At this point, what do you think of the PERSAR method?

32 Creating and Using Review Sheets

Name _____ Grade _____ Date _____

Review

What do each of the letters in PERSAR stand for? Write them here.

During the last lesson you read some material using the PERSAR method. Below, write as many facts as you can recall from that reading.

Creating and Using Reviewing Sheets

Sometimes, your teachers will require you to learn material from a textbook and to prepare for a test on the textbook material without providing you with any review sheets. In such instances, you can create your own review sheets that will help you memorize the material. An effective way to create a review sheet is to use a question and answer format.

Steps for Creating a Review Sheet

1. Create your review sheet at least three days before the test. A week or more ahead of the test would be even better.

2. Read the textbook material a paragraph at a time.

3. When you reread the paragraph, select any facts that are completely new to you.

4. In the question column of your review sheet, write a direct question about each new fact.

5. Write the answer in the answer column.

6. If it's hard to think of a question, just put a *who, what, when, where,* or *why* at the front of the factual statement in the textbook. For example, if the fact reads "Sam Houston was the first president of the republic of Texas," your question should be *"Who* was the first president of the republic of Texas?" or *"Who* was Sam Houston?"

7. If there are many new facts in each paragraph, pick the most important fact or facts and write questions for these. Not every new fact needs to go on your review sheet.

8. If your review covers a lot of material and several topics, keep it organized by making a separate sheet for each topic.

9. When the material covers many textbook pages, write the page number where you found the information in the "Page Number" column.

Practice Round 1

Read the social studies selection below and create a review sheet with eight questions and answers using the format on the next page. Follow the steps listed under the "Steps for Creating a Review Sheet" section.

Alexander the Great was one of the most famous rulers of ancient Greece. His father, King Philip II of Macedonia, had been murdered shortly after he took control of Greece. As a result, Alexander became the king when he was only 20 years old. Young Alexander and his army soon proved their military strength by capturing the city of Thebes. Alexander then had the city completely destroyed, leaving only the house of a famous poet standing. Alexander then set out to conquer more lands. He and his army would go on to conquer Egypt and all of the Middle East, stopping only when he came to the borders of India. Like his father, Alexander died young, at the age of 32. The empire he had built so quickly was divided up among his generals. One of the generals, Ptolemy, became the ruler of Egypt. Cleopatra, the famous Egyptian queen, was one of his descendants. The main result of Alexander's far-reaching conquests was the spread of Greek culture throughout the Middle East. For example, gymnasiums for sports were built in the Middle East by the Greek rulers. Today, many ancient Greek ruins can be found throughout the lands conquered by Alexander the Great.

Review Sheet

Name _____   Subject/Topic _____

Dates Reviewed ___ ___ ___ ___ ___

Page Number	Question	Answer		Correct Responses			

Rules for Using Your Review Sheet

1. At the top of the sheet, under "Dates Reviewed," write in the date each time you study the material.
2. Cover up the "Answer" column and only look at the answer for each question after you have retrieved it or guessed.
3. Each time you get an answer correct, put a check mark in the "Correct Responses" column. Once you have checked an item off as correct, you don't need to review it again until the next time you study the sheet (this is like sorting study cards; see Lesson 29).
4. Keep going over the questions until all of them have been checked off.
5. Create a final review sheet of the items that are always the hardest to remember, and follow all of these rules with this special review sheet.
6. Be sure to study the review sheet on at least three separate days before a test.
7. When someone tests you with the sheet, have that person mark the "Correct Responses" column as you respond correctly.

Practice Round 2

Now practice using the review sheet you created, following the rules above.

How to Study From a Teacher's Review Sheet

Many teachers will provide you with a study guide or review packet prior to an exam. To improve your recall of the teacher's review materials, follow these tips:

1. Start studying the materials as soon as you receive them so that you have an opportunity to review them on at least three separate days before the test.
2. Go through the materials and highlight the information that you don't understand and that has been difficult to remember. Then create a question-and-answer review sheet of your own for this most difficult material. Then follow the Rules for Using Your Review Sheet that are stated on the top of this page.
3. If it's a long packet of review information, start each review on a different page so that the same material is not always in the middle.
4. Test yourself on the material by covering up the answer or information under an item until you have recalled it the best you can. Then check to see if you knew it or answered correctly.
5. Each time you know an item or answer the question correctly, check it off. Then keep reviewing the other items until they are all checked off. Follow this step during each review.
6. If the review materials are not organized very well, reorganize them in a way that makes sense to you.

Assignment

Create a review sheet on material that you are required to read for a class. Or, you may create a review sheet of the most difficult material taken from a study guide a teacher has provided. There is a blank review page in Appendix L. Bring your completed review sheet to the next session.

33 Testing Yourself

Name _____ Grade _____ Date _____

Did you know that taking tests actually helps you learn and remember more information? It's not just because you study for tests. It's because testing forces you to retrieve the information. Every time you retrieve memories, it makes the memory connections stronger. The result is that you will remember information better after you have been tested on it.

You can take advantage of the "testing effect" whenever you study. When you study, don't just read over or repeat information. Test yourself on the material, or have someone else test you. When you do, always answer the question or at least take a guess before you look at the answer. Study cards and review sheets are ideal for testing yourself.

Tips for Self–Testing

1. Always answer the question, even if you have to guess, before looking at or hearing the answer.

2. When someone else is testing you, that person should immediately tell you the correct answer whenever you give an incorrect answer.

3. It's best to use the same testing format your teacher will use. For example, if there will be matching, test yourself with matching.

4. The first time you test yourself should be within 24 hours of the time you first read the information or heard it in class.

5. Try to test yourself on at least three different days before you take the actual test.

6. Do not review the information just before you test yourself on it.

7. If you can remember nothing about the question, be sure that you go back and review that topic before you test yourself on it again.

8. It's not necessary to test yourself on every possible item your teacher might have on the test. Your recall of untested information on a topic will improve simply from testing yourself on related information.

9. Keep track of how well you do when self-testing so you can determine if you are improving with each round of self-testing.

10. People who help you study can simply ask you questions on the material. It's not necessary to actually write out all of the questions.

11. It's okay to use different questions when the material is self-tested a second and third time.

12. When self-testing, you don't need to write up questions or create study cards all the time. Reading something and then covering it up and seeing if you can repeat it to yourself is a simple but effective method of self-testing. For example, you are self-testing spelling whenever you cover up a word and then try to spell it.

Practice

Use either a review sheet or a set of flash cards that you created previously to practice self-testing. Follow the tips above when you do.

34 Study Skills That Help Memory

Name _____ Grade _____ Date _____

Review

During Lesson 31, you selected four facts from a reading selection without using the PERSAR method and four facts when you were using PERSAR. Your trainer will now ask you a question about each fact.

Did you remember the facts studied with PERSAR better than the ones without?

Study Skills

Several of the memory methods and strategies taught in this workbook can also be considered good study skills.

Here are some study skills that will improve your long-term memory for what you study. Check the ones that you usually do.

❑ Before you start to study, get yourself relaxed and try to eliminate some of the stress of the day. One way to do this is to focus on and control your breathing. Slowly fill your lungs completely as you breathe in through your nose and out through your mouth.

❑ Really try to concentrate and focus your attention on what you are studying. You can get information into factual memory better when you are paying attention.

❑ Take frequent breaks, at least once every hour, and more frequently when the material is difficult or there is a lot to remember. The breaks need not be long, just a few minutes. Without breaks, your long-term memory center gets overloaded and you won't remember as much later.

❑ Think about what the information means to you personally. Think about how you might use this skill or knowledge in your daily life.

❑ When you have a test the next day, review the material again just before you go to sleep. While you sleep, your long-term memory center will keep processing that information and you will remember it better the next day.

You will find more study skill suggestions under the section on "Suggestions for Supporting Working Memory During Home Study" in Lesson 22.

Assignment

Which of the above suggestions that you have never done would you like to try this coming week?

Discuss with your trainer the details of how you will try this suggestion. Next week, report to your trainer on how it went.

35 Using Music to Remember

Name _____ Grade _____ Date _____

Have you ever noticed how well you remember songs? Music can be used to memorize facts that are otherwise difficult to remember. Every child learns the ABCs by singing them, and students who have sung the multiplication facts have been able to remember them better. To make your own memorization song, just take a popular song and replace the words with the facts you want to learn.

Share with your trainer any school facts that you have learned by singing them.

Practice

Below is the science lesson that was presented earlier in this workbook. Imagine that you have to memorize how the blood circulates through the body and the heart. First, write a short, simple description of blood circulation on a separate sheet of paper. Then pick a popular tune and try to get the words to match the melody. You may have to revise your wording or pick another tune to make it work. Practice singing the song a few times once you have it put together.

> The heart is an organ that pumps blood through the circulatory system. The heart is divided into four chambers: two upper and two lower. The two upper chambers are called atria, with each one being called an atrium. The lower chambers consist of two ventricles. On each side of the heart, there is one atrium and one ventricle. To trace the flow of blood through the heart, begin with the right atrium, where blood enters as it returns from the body. From the right atrium, the blood is pumped into the right ventricle. From there, it is pumped into a large artery, which takes it to the lungs where it releases carbon dioxide and picks up oxygen. Upon returning to the lungs, the blood enters the left atrium and is pumped into the left ventricle. From the left ventricle blood is pumped out through a large artery called the aorta. Through branching arteries and capillaries, the blood reaches all cells in the body before once again returning to the heart.

> Write the final version of your song here.

36   Review and Reflections

Name _____ Grade _____ Date _____

Sing the song you created last time about blood circulation.

   Did you remember all of it?

1. What are two important things to do when using study cards to memorize?

2. Why does elaboration, or thinking about the information, help you remember the information better?

3. What question should you ask and answer when you want to use elaboration?

4. When reading to remember, you should do the PERSAR steps. What does each letter of PERSAR stand for?

5. Below, draw and label the columns you should use when creating a review sheet.

6. On how many different days should you study a review sheet before a test?

7. Why does testing yourself improve your memory for the material?

8. Write about a time your memory has been better because you used one of the methods you learned in a memory training session.

9. Write about a time within the last couple of weeks when you could not remember something you really wanted to remember.

10. Which of the memory strategies you have learned do you like the most?

11. Which of the memory strategies do not seem to work that well for you?

37 Remembering to Do Things

Name _____ Grade _____ Date _____

Remembering to do something in the future is a challenge for everyone. There are many things we must remember to do at certain point in time. Examples include remembering someone's birthday, remembering to bring materials for a special activity, remembering to keep a doctor's appointment, remembering to take medicine, remembering to do regular chores, and remembering all the school assignments that need to be completed. We all forget to do things we really wanted to do, even when those things are very important to us. Part of growing up is learning to take responsibility for getting things done on time. When we forget to do things, it's not just due to a memory weakness. It's often due to poor planning. In other words, we need to set up a system of reminders so that we don't forget to do things on time.

Practice Round 1

The most common way that people remember to do things is to make a plan, write it down, carry it with them, and constantly check it until everything is finished. Imagine you are going Christmas shopping for friends. In the space below, create an organized list of two gifts that you plan to buy for each of four friends. For each gift, write down the store where you plan to purchase it.

<u>Names</u>   <u>Gifts</u>   <u>Stores</u>

Other Tips for Remembering to Do Things

Check the ones that you have done.

❏ Plan for what needs to be done and make appropriate arrangements for it.

❏ Write things down in an appointment calendar or an electronic calendar.

❏ Always carry your electronic or paper calendar with you.

❏ Set a reminder alarm or message on a cell phone, computer, or similar electronic device.

❏ Place objects in an unusual location where you will notice them.

❏ Place objects you want to remember in the same location (known as a "memory spot"), such as placing items near the door you will exit when leaving home.

❏ Carry a checklist of things to do with you.

Pick one of the above methods that you have not done before and write it down below.

Now, discuss with your trainer how you might start using this method. Next week, report to your trainer on how it went.

Practice Round 2

People use calendars for more than remembering school assignments. People who really want to remember things use a calendar to write down everything that is going to happen and everything they need to do. They then carry the calendar with them at all times and check it throughout the day so that they don't forget anything. For each of the events below, make up a date and time(s) the event will occur. Then fill in the information properly on the one-month calendar below. Be sure to write in the times the event will occur.

❏ A friend's birthday party that you have been invited to

❏ A playoff game that you plan to attend (tickets must be purchased in advance)

❏ Practice for a school event that you must attend on three different dates

❏ A dental appointment

❏ Taking out the garbage each week

❏ A date by which you must pay for something

❏ A time you will talk with a friend online

Sun	Mon	Tue	Wed	Thu	Fri	Sat
						1
2	3	4	5	6	7	8
9	10	11	12	13	14	15
16	17	18	19	20	21	22
23	24	25	26	27	28	29
30	31					

Assignment

Next time, bring the calendar or device you will be using from now on.

38 Memory Aids

Name _____ Grade _____ Date _____

Calendar Practice

Show your trainer the calendar or electronic device you have been using to record all upcoming events. Then update your calendar by entering everything you can think of that needs to be added.

Memory Aids

Knowing that we can't remember everything, it's a smart idea to use memory aids. Below is a list of memory aids other than a calendar. Check the ones you use.

❏ Timers or alarms   ❏ Post-it notes   ❏ Checklists

❏ Memory journals   ❏ Computer or cell reminders   ❏ To-do lists

❏ Memory notebook   ❏ Personal digital assistant   ❏ Memory spot

Now, pick a memory aid that you would like to start using and discuss with your trainer how you will use it. Write your plan for using it below.

For what materials or situations will you use this aid?

When will you use this aid, including how often you will use it or check it?

What other ideas do you have for using this aid?

39 Creating and Using a Memory Book

Name _____ Grade _____ Date _____

Some people with memory problems overcome these problems by creating and using a "memory book." People who have a memory book carry it with them at all times so that they can add information and check on information whenever they need to, which is usually several times a day. Although a memory book may include a calendar, it is much more than that. Here are the different types of information that might go into a memory book:

1. Pictures of people with their names and who they are written underneath.
2. Names, addresses, and phone numbers of people you want to remember. Instead of arranging them alphabetically by name, arrange them by what they do or by how you remember them. For example, if you keep forgetting the track coach's name, you would file the name and phone number under "T" for track coach or under "C" for coach.
3. Directions for step-by-step procedures that you do regularly but have a hard time remembering. For example, you might write down the steps for finding and using a program on the Internet.
4. Your school class schedule, so that you can check to see what comes next and exactly when it begins and ends.
5. A list of chores that you need to do daily or weekly. For those that involve steps, include all the steps that are required.
6. A record of all phone calls with adults and friends. For these, write down who you talked with, the date and time, and most importantly what the other person said and what you said.
7. A record of important events and information. For example, perhaps you went for a dental appointment without a parent. As you leave the dentist's office, you might write down what the dentist said so that you can accurately report the information to a parent.
8. Descriptions and steps for how to do certain kinds of homework and projects. For example, you might have a list of steps to follow for writing and editing a project.
9. Directions for how to get somewhere. For example, which city buses to take when riding public transportation on your own. You might even put some maps into a memory book.

10. Descriptions of memory methods and strategies, including all the steps involved. You might also add what types of materials and situations each memory strategy works for.
11. A daily journal of memory successes and failures.
12. A diary of what happened each day.

Assignment

Get the materials you need and organize a memory book. Put in dividers for the sections you will have. Then start using it by entering information for each section. In the future, bring it to each memory training session.

40 Keyword

Name _____ Grade _____ Date _____

Practice Round 1

Use repetition to memorize the meaning of the following Spanish words:

Bolso = Purse   Reina = Queen

Mapache = Raccoon   Llover = Rain

Listo = Ready   Quitar = To remove

Keyword

Keyword is a memory strategy that can be used to remember new vocabulary words, new foreign language words, and other facts, such as state capitals. There are three steps to the keyword method.

Step One

When you must learn a new word, first think of a word that the new word sounds like. For example, the Spanish word "pato" sounds like "pot." With longer words, you only need to connect the first part of the new word with a word you already know. For example, "Madison" might remind you of "Mad." The word the new word sounds like is called the *keyword*.

Step Two

Take the keyword, such as "pot" for "pato," and create a picture in your mind that combines the keyword and the meaning of the new word. For example, the Spanish word pato means duck. Because the keyword is pot, you might create an image of a duck in a pot. This method works best when there is interaction between the two parts of the image or the image is funny (see the picture on the next page). So, you might picture a duck splashing in a pot. Keep your picture simple and focused on the two important elements, such as the duck and the pot.

Now you try one. Take the first part of the Spanish word "bandera." Does "ban" remind you of the English word "banana?" Bandera means flag. So you need to combine banana and flag into a funny image. Draw a picture of your image alongside the duck above.

Step Three

When you need to recall what the new word means, think of the keyword first. That is, first think of the word the new word sounds like. When you do, the picture you created will come to mind and you will know what the new word means.

Practice Round 2

Use the keyword method to memorize the meaning of the Spanish words below. For each word, first tell your trainer the keyword and then describe the image you created with the keyword and the definition.

Gritar = Scream	Mudar = Shed	Zapato = Shoe
Palo = Stick	Equipo = Team	Carpa = Tent

Practice Round 3

Keyword can also be used for words that are paired, such as names of states and their capitals. In this case, both the name of the state and the capital will have keywords. For example, the capital of Kansas is Topeka. A keyword for Kansas is "cans," and a keyword for Topeka is "toe." An image that combines them might be of a boy with a big toe kicking cans. When asked to recall the capital, you would first think of "cans." When you see the boy with a big toe kicking them, you will associate "toe" with Topeka, and know the answer. Try using keyword to memorize the pairs below. Share the keywords and images with your trainer as you do each one.

Colorado: Denver	Florida: Tallahassee	Oregon: Salem
Ohio: Columbus	Wisconsin: Madison	Connecticut: Hartford

How do you feel about the keyword strategy?

Why do you think it works?

Assignment

Think of a class where you have to memorize vocabulary. Bring the vocabulary words to the next lesson so that you can try memorizing them with keyword.

41 Taking Class Notes

Name _____ Grade _____ Date _____

Taking Notes

Listening to a teacher and taking notes at the same time can overload your working memory. When this happens, you may not hear everything the teacher says, may not understand something the teacher says, may not copy the notes correctly, or may not be able to write down all the needed information. Some students are allowed to ask their teachers for copies of the outline or notes. Even if a teacher provides you with the outline or notes, you should still write down some additional information.

Practice Round 1

The first way to make note-taking quicker and easier is to use abbreviations. There are formal abbreviations, such as U.S. for United States, but almost any word can be abbreviated simply by writing the first few letters of the word. Abbreviations are especially helpful for long words and words you don't know how to spell. Just put a period after the abbreviation so that you know it's an abbreviation. Write an abbreviation for each of the following words:

Equipment

History

Empire

Forest

Preparation

Medical

Capitol

Spaniards

Practice Round 2

Another way to reduce the load on your working memory during note-taking is to create and use a code for frequently used words. This method is sometimes referred to as *personal shorthand*. In creating a code, use the first one or two letters of the word to represent the word. Write the code at the top of your notes so that you know what each letter stands for. For example, if your history teacher is talking about the Puritans in New England, you might use "P" for Puritans and "NE" for New England. You can also use symbols for basic words, such as "&" for "and" (see Appendix J for some basic shorthand examples). Create your own code for the following words:

Mayflower =   Indians =   Winter =

Plymouth Rock =   Thanksgiving =   Turkey =

When you read and review your notes after class, you should fill in the full words for any codes and abbreviations. You especially should write out the words for any codes or abbreviations you made up or used for the first time. Remember to leave some space after abbreviations and codes so that you have room to do this. The other option is to make a key for abbreviations and codes at the top of your notes.

Practice Round 3

You should now take notes as your trainer gives a talk on how to plan for a wilderness canoe trip. A few subheadings for the presentation are provided below. You should fill in the details under each section so that your notes provide you with all of the important information. First, fill in the code you will use for these words that will occur frequently during the talk.

Canoe =   Paddles =   Food =   Equipment =

If you notice other words that keep coming up, abbreviate or code them and then write them here when the talk is over.

Efficient Materials

Safety Equipment

Food and Water

Reviewing, Editing, and Adding to Your Notes After Class

Your notes will be more complete, memorable, and valuable if you review and add to them as soon as possible after class. Do the things below during any study time you have during the day, or as soon as you get home from school. Be sure to do them within 24 hours of taking the original notes. To do these things, you need to allow room by skipping lines while you are taking notes in class.

1. Write in the complete words for any abbreviations you created while taking the notes. If the same abbreviation is used repeatedly, write the abbreviation and its corresponding word at the top of your notes.

2. Write in the full word for any coded word or shorthand that you do not immediately recognize.

3. While you still remember them, write down any details that were discussed but that you didn't have time to write down.

4. Underline or circle anything in your notes that is confusing or incomplete, and ask a classmate or the teacher about it as soon as you have a chance.

5. Consider how the information relates to you personally. For example, think about whether you agree with the ideas in the notes. Write your opinions and reactions in the margins next to the ideas.

Now do these five steps for the notes you just took on planning a wilderness canoe trip.

Additional Note-Taking Tips

1. Copy anything the teacher writes on the board or screen, but also write down more than what the teacher has written out.

2. Focus on writing down the main points, and leave space to fill in missing details later. If you have the main points and some of the details written down, you will be able to remember other details when you review your notes after class.

3. When the teacher emphasizes or repeats information, these are clues that the information is important and that you should write it down.

Assignment

Try these note-taking methods in a class in which you are required to take notes. Create a code for words that are frequently used, and also use abbreviations. Write these on the top of your notes before or after note-taking. Also, review and add to your notes as soon as possible after class. Show the notes you take using these methods to your trainer next time you meet.

42   Studying From Class Notes

Name _____ Grade _____ Date _____

Review

With your trainer, look over notes that you recently took in a class. What new methods of note-taking have you tried?

How to Study From Class Notes

1. If your notes are messy and hard to read, rewrite them.
2. Reorganize the information in your notes in a way that makes more sense to you. For example, you might convert a traditional outline into a graphic organizer. Or, you could regroup all the information in your notes by topic.
3. Read through your notes and highlight the most important information.
4. Circle anything you don't understand and ask your teacher or a classmate about it.
5. If your notes contain vocabulary and other facts that you must memorize, convert these to study cards with a question on the front and the answer on the back, or make a review sheet with questions and answers in separate columns.
6. Create a review sheet of hard-to-remember information. Each time you review your notes, write on this sheet any information that you did not immediately recognize or remember. Spend extra time reviewing the information on this sheet.
7. Don't wait until the night before a test to study from your notes. You should study and review from your notes on at least three different days prior to a test.

Practice

Using notes from one of your classes, highlight the most important facts and information that you need to memorize. Then, using the question-and-answer format on the next page, create a review sheet for at least seven important facts that you highlighted.

Name _____ Subject/Topic _____

Dates Reviewed ____ ____ ____ ____ ____

Page Number	Question	Answer	Correct Responses					

43 Scheduling Reviews

Name _____ Grade _____ Date _____

Review

Your trainer will now ask you the meaning of the Spanish words that you studied a couple lessons ago using the repetition method.

Your trainer will now ask you the meaning of the Spanish words you studied using the keyword method. First, think of what English word the Spanish word sounds like or reminds you of. Then, think of the image. The image will give you a clue about the meaning of the Spanish word.

Your trainer will now ask you what the capitals are for the states you memorized with keyword. Again, first recall what word the state's name reminds you of.

How well did you remember the definitions and capitals? Does the keyword strategy help?

Scheduling Reviews

Students who are serious about trying to memorize material for school will often review that material several times a day or every day for many days. Yet, memory scientists have proven that spreading out reviews actually allows us to remember more of the information and remember it for longer periods of time. The explanation for this puzzling fact is that when it's too easy to retrieve information, our memory connections are not strengthened. For example, when you review a vocabulary list several times a day, the answers will come easily. However, if you wait to review the list until you are starting to forget it and have to make an effort to retrieve the answers, that effort makes the memory connections stronger.

This does not mean that you can wait until the night before a test to "cram" for it. That approach is not effective either. The best way to review is to start early, so that you can space out the review sessions, with longer and longer periods of time between reviews. In order for this system to work, you need to start studying the material far enough in advance of the test, at least a week in advance. This takes some planning and sticking to the review schedule you have set up. For unit exams in many classes, the teacher will keep adding new information right up to the day of the test. In such situations, you will need to keep adding information to your review materials, or set up different review schedules for different sets of material. Below is the review schedule that is recommended.

First Review

Your first review session should be the day after your first exposure to the new information, such as the day after you read about it, hear it in class, or create study cards or a review sheet. This means you should read the material and create study cards and review sheets as early as possible.

Second Review

Your second review should be two days after the first review. By this time you will have forgotten some of the material, but that's okay. Just be sure to try hard to remember, and take a guess before you look at or are told the answer. Use the sorting technique (see Lessons 29 and 32) so that you go over the forgotten items at least a couple of times.

Third Review

Ideally, the third review should be from four days to one week after the second review. If you don't have that much time, try for a two-day break between reviews. Apply the same rules recommended for the second review.

Final Review

The final review should be the night before the test or sometime during the day of the test. As suggested in Lesson 29, during this review, you should focus on the items that have been the hardest to remember. If you have more than one set of review materials, you will review all of the sets at this time.

Practice

On the next page is a calendar for you to fill in your review plan for the following situation. You will have a unit exam on the 26th. The unit exam will cover Chapters 1 and 2. You can create your review materials for Chapter 1 on the 10th, but you will not be able to complete the review materials for Chapter 2 until the 21st. Plan and write in separate review schedules for Chapters 1 and 2. Follow the recommendations above.

Sun	Mon	Tue	Wed	Thu	Fri	Sat
						1
2	3	4	5	6	7	8
9	10	11	12	13	14	15
16	17	18	19	20	21	22
23	24	25	26	27	28	29
30	31					

Now, using your own assignment calendar, set up a review plan for one of your actual upcoming tests. Even if you don't know the exact date of your next exam, you can still create your study materials as soon as possible and set up a review schedule for them. If you want to see your test scores improve, follow the review schedule that you set up.

Assignment

For your remaining memory training sessions, bring your assignment calendar with you so that your trainer can help you set up a review schedule for other upcoming tests.

Conclusion of Kim's Story

As the memory training continued, Kim learned more about how her memory worked. She began to realize that she could have some control over her memory, and this made her feel more confident and less anxious and frustrated about everything that she had to study. Of the latest memory strategies that she learned, Kim especially liked making and using study cards and using visual imagery. Kim's organization of her notes and other study materials had improved during the training, but she still had a lot of difficulty planning and following through with a review schedule. Some of the memory strategies actually saved her time, but others, such as elaboration and creating review sheets, were time consuming. When she complained about having to spend more time studying, her trainer reminded her that getting information solidly into memory takes time and effort.

At the end of the memory training program, Kim was asked to reflect on what she had learned. These are some of her actual comments:

➤ "Most of my memory problems come from how much effort and energy I put in."
➤ "Memorizing words the old way was so slow and time consuming."
➤ "The method I like is pictures, because it's fun to create funny ones to help memorize."
➤ "When using strategies, memory is powerful."

After completing the memory training program, Kim went on to get the best school grades she had ever had.

LESSON 44 Teaching the Information

Name _____ Grade _____ Date _____

Review

Explain to your trainer why spreading out reviews makes your memory stronger than doing several reviews in one day.

Teaching to Remember

Whenever you have to teach something to someone else, it strengthens your learning, understanding, and memory of that material. Even though you might never have to formally teach something, following some of the suggestions below can really strengthen your memory for difficult-to-remember facts and information.

Suggestions

1. Organize the information as if you had to do a presentation on it. For example, you might make an outline of what you have read about a topic.
2. Think about how you would explain information and ideas to someone else.
3. Explain to your parents something new that you learned in school.
4. When you study with a friend, take turns teaching and explaining the material.
5. When you study with a friend, make up questions and test your friend.
6. Help someone else memorize information.
7. Volunteer to tutor a younger student in a subject that you have a difficult time learning and remembering. For example, if remembering math facts is difficult for you, try teaching them to a younger student.

Practice

Read the brief lesson on blood circulation found in Lesson 6. Develop a plan for how you would teach this to your classmates if you had to do a presentation on it. Explain to your trainer how you would do the following and then write a summary for each:

Organize and explain the information

Help classmates memorize it

Test them on it

Assignment

Pick one of the suggestions from the list of seven on the previous page. Try it this coming week and report back to your memory trainer about how it went.

45 Using Context Cues

Name _____ Grade _____ Date _____

Context Cues

The factual information we learn in class is often connected with other, more personal memories. That is why recalling some personal memories may help jog your memory of facts you are trying to retrieve. If you are taking a test in the same classroom where you learned the information, look around the classroom and try to remember what was happening on the days the teacher was talking about the material on the test. Try to visualize the scene, what the teacher was doing, and how you felt at the time. If you are taking the test in a different classroom, close your eyes and picture the classroom where you learned the material. Then try to remember as much as you can about what was happening during the lessons you are being tested on. This nonfactual information that you are trying to recall is referred to as *context cues*. Recalling context cues will help you retrieve some hard-to-remember facts that you learned in that context (a place or situation, such as a classroom). Below is a list of context cues that you should try to recall about the days you were learning the material in class.

> ➤ What the room looked like
> ➤ Any special objects that were in the room
> ➤ Who was there and what they were doing
> ➤ What the teacher was doing or saying
> ➤ The sounds and smells in the room
> ➤ What you were doing at that time
> ➤ How you felt at that time

Practice

Think about a class you had this past week. Go through the list above, tell your trainer as many context cues as you can recall, and then write them below.

Assignment

Try using this method the next time you take a classroom test, especially when the test is not in the same room where you learned the material.

46 Improving Recall During Tests

Name _____ Grade _____ Date _____

Very often, we "know" something but can't remember it during a test. The suggestions below will help you remember more information during a test. Most of the suggestions work because they will help your retrieval processes "find" the information that you don't immediately recall.

Do a Final Review

Just before you take a test, do a brief, final review of the hardest-to-remember information. The hard-to-remember items are the ones you could not remember each time you did a review. You should have put these hard-to-remember items on a special review sheet (see Lessons 29, 32, and 42).

Think of Context Cues

Before you look at the test questions, close your eyes and try to recall as many context cues as you can from the classes in which the material was taught (see Lesson 45).

Elaborate

Use elaboration when you come to a difficult question you don't remember the answer to. Elaboration involves thinking about what you do know about the topic (see Lesson 30). For example, at first you might not remember the answer to the question, "In which colony did the first battle of the American Revolutionary War take place?" Take some time to remember other facts about the Revolutionary War; you might also run through the list of colonies in your mind. Thinking about the topic in more ways than one will increase the chances that you will remember the answer to the question.

Other Testing Suggestions

1. As soon as the test begins, write somewhere on the test any formulas, definitions, lists, or details that you believe you will forget within a few minutes. For example, if you've had to memorize a list of science facts, write them somewhere on the test or your answer sheet before reading and attempting any test questions.

2. Look over the whole test and some of the questions before you begin to answer any of them. This preview will activate the proper memory files.

3. Underline the key words or phrases in the test questions so that you focus on and remember what the question is asking.

4. When you come to a test question you can remember absolutely nothing about, skip it and come back to it after you finish the other questions.

5. If you used a memory strategy such as keyword or some other strategy to study, use that strategy now to recall the answers.

6. Don't rush your memory when it's working. Give it some time to retrieve the information you want.

7. Give your memory a chance to "recognize" the answer. For example, if you know that the vocabulary term you want begins with the letter "t," then start running through words that begin with "t" in your mind. You will probably recognize the correct word when you come to it.

8. Don't change your answers unless you are absolutely sure that your first response is wrong. Your unconscious memory will guide you to answers without your being able to understand or remember why they are correct; so, it's safer to stick with your first answer.

9. When writing an essay on a test, organize your ideas by doing a brief outline before you start writing. This process will reduce working memory overload and also help you remember information you should include in the essay.

10. Don't let nervousness and anxiety get the upper hand. Test anxiety really interferes with memory recall. If you get very anxious, calm yourself down by controlling your breathing (see Lesson 34) and picturing yourself outside the testing room in a place you enjoy.

Practice

You will now be tested on some material that was learned during the lesson on elaboration (the lesson in which you practiced answering the "Why does this make sense" question). Use some of the methods discussed above (except doing a final review) to help you remember the answers. Write in the answers.

1. The Mekong River, which begins in Tibet, flows into which sea?

2. What two things were found in King Tut's tomb?

3. Which city has the worst air pollution in the world?

4. What did the Mongolian horsemen create?

5. What is the wide open land in Australia called?

6. Who were the first ancient people to have a 12-month calendar?

7. Which invention caused universities to stop teaching memorization methods?

8. During what season of the year did so many men in Napoleon's army die while retreating from Russia?

9. What does it mean to say that a king rules by divine right?

10. Which ancient civilization built 50,000 miles of roads made out of stone and gravel?

Which methods did you use to recall some of the hard-to remember-information?

Assignment

Try using some of these test-taking strategies the next time you take a challenging test. Report back to your trainer on whether you think any of the methods helped you recall information you needed to answer the test questions.

47 Selecting, Modifying, and Combining Strategies

Name _____ Grade _____ Date _____

Memory strategies become even more powerful when you combine them. For example, the combination of repeating and picturing information is more effective than either method alone. You can also adapt and modify strategies so that they work better for you. Below is a list of the memory strategies covered in this workbook. Have you adapted or modified any of these as you have used them? If so, explain to your trainer what you did.

Practice Round 1

Pick at least two different pairings of strategies and explain how you would use them in combination.

Repetition	Chunking
Putting Words Into Sentences and Stories	Picturing Verbal Information
Naming and Describing What You See	Grouping Words by Category
Imagining Yourself in the Scene	Using Locations to Remember
Pegword	Using Study Cards
Thinking About the Information	PERSAR for Reading
Creating and Using Review Sheets	Testing Yourself
Creating and Using a Memory Book	Using Music to Remember
Studying From Class Notes	Scheduling Reviews
Teaching the Information	Keyword
Using Context Cues	

Practice Round 2

One of the challenges of using memory strategies is picking the right strategy for the job. For each situation below, pick one or more strategies that you think would be effective and write them in.

1. You must memorize information from material you read on your own.

2. You have to learn some foreign language vocabulary.

3. You need to remember a shopping list, and you have no paper on which to write it.

4. You want to remember a literature selection for a quiz tomorrow.

5. You need to memorize the spelling of some words.

6. You need to prepare for a final exam that covers a few chapters.

After you selected a strategy, how will you know if it's working?

If it's not working, what should you do?

48 Test on Memory and Strategies

Name _____ Grade _____ Date _____

Directions

Answer the questions without looking back at the information. After you have completed the test, you can look up information that you have forgotten. The lesson in which the answer can be found is provided after each question.

1. In long-term memory, information is usually stored in either a verbal form or in a _____ form. (Lesson 3)

2. There are two main long-term memory systems; one is for factual information and the other is for _____ information. (Lesson 3)

3. What is one type of memory in which you have a weakness? (Lesson 4)

4. Is repetition better for long-term memory or short-term memory? (Lesson 11)

5. When you play the card game in which you have to remember the previous cards, which type of memory can the card game strengthen? (Lesson 20)

6. What does dual encoding mean, and why does it improve your ability to recall the information? (Lesson 23)

7. Why does grouping words by category help your memory for those words? (Lesson 24)

8. When you link things to remember with objects in your room, what will make those images easier to remember? (Lesson 26)

9. How should you sort flash cards whenever you study them? (Lesson 29)

10. When you ask and answer a certain question, it forces you to think about the new information you are reading or studying. What is that question? (Lesson 30)

11. When you want to better understand and remember what you read, what is the first step? (Lesson 31)

12. One way to make sure you are actually retrieving the new information you are trying to learn and remember is to _____ yourself. (Lesson 33)

13. At home, what is one thing you can do to make sure you remember to take something when you leave the house? (Lesson 37)

14. If you create a memory book, what is one type of information you could write in it? (Lesson 39)

15. When trying to remember a word that you studied with keyword, what should you try to remember first, the image you created or the word it sounds like? (Lesson 40)

16. When you review your notes shortly after a class, what is one thing you should add to your notes? (Lesson 41)

17. When studying from class notes that you took, what is something that you can do to better memorize that information? (Lesson 42)

18. True or False: It is better to have longer and longer breaks between your reviews of material, instead of reviewing the same material every day. (Lesson 43)

19. If you take a test outside of the classroom for that subject, what is one thing you should try to think of before answering the questions? (Lesson 45)

20. What is another thing you should do when you cannot remember the answer to a test question? (Lesson 46)

49 Plans for Using Memory Strategies

Name _____ Grade _____ Date _____

Directions

Look at the list of memory strategies below and:

1. Put a + beside the ones that work best for you.
2. Put a − beside the ones that do not seem to work well for you.
3. Put an *H* beside the ones that you plan to use to improve your memory for what you need to remember outside of school.
4. Put an *S* beside the ones that you plan to use to improve your memory for what you need to learn and memorize for school.
5. For each strategy you mark with an *S*, write in an example of a class for which you would use it.

<u>Class Example</u>

___ Repetition
___ Chunking
___ Putting Words Into Sentences and Stories
___ Picturing Verbal Information
___ Naming and Describing What You See
___ Grouping Words by Category
___ Imagining Yourself in the Scene
___ Using Locations to Remember Information
___ Pegword
___ Using Study Cards
___ Thinking About the Information
___ Remembering What You Read (PERSAR)
___ Creating and Using Review Sheets
___ Testing Yourself
___ Using Music to Remember
___ Remembering to Do Things
___ Memory Aids

___ Creating and Using a Memory Book

___ Keyword

___ Taking Class Notes

___ Studying From Class Notes

___ Scheduling Reviews

___ Teaching the Information

___ Using Context Cues

___ Improving Recall During Tests

___ Selecting, Modifying, and Combining Strategies

What other plans do you have for using any of the new memory strategies that you learned?

50 Evaluation of Training

Name _____ Grade _____ Date _____

Directions

The statements below are about all of the memory training sessions combined. Circle the choice that best describes what you think about each statement.

1. I learned a lot about how everybody's memory works.
   I disagree   I don't know   I agree

2. I learned a lot about how my memory works.
   I disagree   I don't know   I agree

3. I enjoyed coming to the training sessions.
   I disagree   I don't know   I agree

4. My memory trainer did a good job.
   I disagree   I don't know   I agree

5. Since the training began, my short-term memory has improved.
   I disagree   I don't know   I agree

6. Since the training began, my working memory has improved.
   I disagree   I don't know   I agree

7. Since the training began, my long-term memory has improved.
   I disagree   I don't know   I agree

8. I learned some new and helpful memory strategies.
   I disagree   I don't know   I agree

9. I am doing better on classroom tests because of this memory training.
   I disagree   I don't know   I agree

10. The time it takes to do these new memory strategies is well worth it.

    I disagree   I don't know   I agree

11. I need to practice some of the memory strategies more, so that I know how to use them.

    I disagree   I don't know   I agree

12. I accomplished the goals I had set for this memory training.

    I disagree   I don't know   I agree

13. Since the training began, I am more in control of my memory.

    I disagree   I don't know   I agree

14. I have practiced some memory exercises and strategies at home.

    I disagree   I don't know   I agree

15. I now frequently use one or more of the new memory strategies when I study.

    I disagree   I don't know   I agree

16. What are two things you liked most about this memory training program?

17. What are two things you liked least about this memory training program?

18. What are the two most important things that you learned about memory or memory strategies?

19. What suggestions do you have for improving this memory training program?

20. Please write any other comments that you would like to make.

APPENDIXES

Practice Schedule and Materials

The number of recommended practice rounds is the minimum most students will need. The actual amount of practice and review required for mastery and generalization will vary considerably. Training should continue until the student understands the applications of the method and has demonstrated successful, independent use outside of the training sessions.

Lower Level

Exercise or Strategy	Minimum Number of Practice Rounds	Materials
Lesson 11: Cumulative Repetition	5	Words lists from Internet generator found at: www.math.yorku.ca/SCS/Online/paivio
Lesson 12: Repeating Written Information	2	Words lists from Internet generator or Appendix D
Lesson 13: Repetition With Spelling	3	Student's spelling words
Lesson 14: Chunking	3	Random digits and word lists from Internet generator
Lesson 16: Chunking With Spelling Repetition and Chunking Combined	3 3	Student's spelling words Student's spelling words
Lesson 17: Sentences and Stories	3	Word lists from Internet generator
Lesson 19: Arithmetic Exercise	10 minutes 4 times weekly for 6 weeks	Arithmetic flash cards and data form in Appendix B
Lesson 20: Card Game (*N*-back)	10 minutes 4 times weekly for 6 weeks	Deck of playing cards and data form in Appendix B
Lesson 21: Visual-Spatial Game	10 minutes 4 times weekly for 4 weeks	Visual-spatial grids from Appendix I and data form in Appendix B
Lesson 22: Picturing Information	5	Word lists from Internet generator

(Continued)

Exercise or Strategy	Minimum Number of Practice Rounds	Materials
Lesson 23: Naming Information	3	Small objects available in classroom
Lesson 24: Grouping Words	3	Appendix G
Lesson 25: Imagining Self in Scene	3	Literature or social studies text or Appendix F
Lesson 26: Loci	3	Science or social studies facts or Appendix F
Lesson 27: Pegword	3	Shopping lists (Appendix H)
Lesson 29: Study Cards	5	Science or social studies facts or Appendix D
Lesson 30: Elaboration	5	Literature, science, or social studies text or Appendix F
Lesson 31: PRSAR	5	Literature, science, or social studies text
Lesson 32: Review Sheets	5	Appendix L, social studies, or science text or Appendix F
Lesson 33: Self-Testing	3	Flash cards and review sheets from previous lessons
Lesson 35: Using Music	2	Science or social studies text
Lesson 37: Remembering to Do Things	As needed	Assignment calendar
Lesson 39: Memory Book	As needed	Notebook

Upper Level

Exercise or Strategy	Minimum Number of Practice Rounds	Materials
Lesson 11: Cumulative Repetition	2	Words lists from Internet generator found at: www.math.yorku.ca/SCS/Online/paivio
Lesson 14: Chunking	2	Random digits and word lists from Internet generator
Lesson 19: Arithmetic Exercise	10 minutes 4 times weekly for 6 weeks	Arithmetic flash cards and data form in Appendix B
Lesson 20: Card Game (N-back)	10 minutes 4 times weekly for 6 weeks	Deck of playing cards and data form in Appendix B

Exercise or Strategy	Minimum Number of Practice Rounds	Materials
Lesson 22: Picturing Information	2	Word lists from Internet generator
Lesson 24: Grouping Words	2	Appendix G
Lesson 25: Imagining Self in Scene	2	Literature or social studies text
Lesson 26: Loci	3	Science or social studies facts or Appendix F
Lesson 27: Pegword	2	Shopping lists (Appendix H)
Lesson 29: Study Cards	3	Science or social studies facts or Appendix D
Lesson 30: Elaboration	5	Literature, science, or social studies text or Appendix F
Lesson 31: PERSAR	4	Literature, science, or social studies text
Lesson 32: Review Sheets	3	Appendix L, social studies, or science text or Appendix F
Lesson 33: Self-Testing	2	Flash cards and review sheets from previous lessons
Lesson 37: Remembering to Do Things	As needed	Assignment calendar
Lesson 39: Memory Book	As needed	Notebook
Lesson 40: Keyword	4	Appendixes C, D, and E
Lesson 42: Studying From Notes	3	Student's class notes
Lesson 43: Scheduling Reviews	5	Assignment calendar
Lesson 44: Teaching the Information	1	Student's class notes
Lesson 45: Context Cues	2	None

B Data Collection Forms

Non-Strategic Versus Strategic Memorization*

Name _____ Grade _____ Date _____

Date	Lesson, Strategy, or Classroom Test	Non-Strategic Percentage Correct	Strategic Percentage
	Lesson 9	(Part I)	(Part II)
	Lesson 11	(Round 1)	(Round 2)
	Lesson 14		
	Lesson 17	(Repetition and Chunking)	(Sentences)
	Lesson 17	(Repetition and Chunking)	(Stories)
	Lesson 22	(Round 1)	(Round 2)
	Lesson 23	(Round 1)	(Round 2)
	Lesson 24	(Round 1)	(Round 2)
	Lesson 30	(Round 1)	(Round 2)
	Lesson 30	(Round 1)	(Round 2)
	Lesson 31		
	Lesson 40 (Upper Level Only)		
	Other Lesson or Assignment		
	Other Lesson or Assignment		
	Other Lesson or Assignment		
	Classroom Tests		
	Classroom Tests		
	Classroom Tests		
	Classroom Tests		

*(Non-strategic are simple methods the student has been using; strategic methods are the ones taught in this workbook.)

Working Memory Arithmetic Exercise (Lesson 19)

Name _____ Grade _____ Date _____

Date	Type of Arithmetic Flash Cards Used	Highest Span

Working Memory *N*–Back Card Game (Lesson 20)

Name _____ Grade _____ Date _____

Date	Beginning *N*-Back Level	Number of Rounds	Highest *N*-Back

Short-Term Memory Visual-Spatial Game (Lesson 21)

Name _____ Grade _____ Date _____

Date	Size of Playing Grid	# of Red & Black Chips	# Correct

Spanish and French Vocabulary

Spanish Vocabulary

Dolor = Ache
Manzana = Apple
Pizarra = Blackboard
Pluma = Feather
Flor = Flower
Caballo = Horse
Patear = To kick
Tapa = Lid
Carne = Meat
Gente = People

Bellota = Acorn
Tia = Aunt
Coche = Car
Pie = Foot
Heno = Hay
Tinta = Ink
Dama = Lady
Buscar = To look
Red = Net
Cartero = Mailman

Contestar = To answer
Campana = Bell
Payaso = Clown
Bombero = Fireman
Corneta = Horn
Saltar = To jump
Lamer = To lick
Comida = Meal
Cubo = Pail
Tirar = To pull

French Vocabulary

Pain = Bread
Chaise = Chair
Hiver = Winter
Nager = To swim
Poisson = Fish
Rhume = Cold
Vache = Cow
Champ = Field
Marché = Market
Glacé = Ice cream

Bras = Arm
Fort = Strong
Jambe = Leg
Orage = Storm
Ranger = To clean up
Sang = Blood
Fer = Iron
Chariot = Shopping cart
Appeller = To call
Manteau = Coat

Canard = Duck
Gras = Fat
Lait = Milk
Plage = Beach
Rein = Kidney
Sel = Salt
Gorge = Throat
Gare = Train station
Banc = Bench
Tard = Late

D English Vocabulary

Lower Level Vocabulary

Agenda = Schedule

Ajar = Partly open

Amity = Friendship

Badger = To tease

Ballad = Song

Brink = Edge

Candor = Truthfulness

Cherub = Angel

Cede = To give up

Deity = God

Dell = Small valley

Don = To put on

Excise = To cut out

Faction = A group

Falter = Stumble

Haven = Safe place

Kin = A relative

Mammoth = Huge

Mimic = To copy

Obese = Very fat

Pesky = Annoying

Purge = To clean out

Rabid = Violent

Raze = Destroy

Rend = To tear

Sage = A wise person

Sear = To burn

Skiff = Small boat

Stout = Strong

Void = Empty

Upper Level Vocabulary

Acerbic = Sour

Adroit = Skillful

Antipathy = Dislike

Behest = A command

Blithe = Cheerful

Burgeon = To expand

Capricious = Unpredictable

Chagrin = Humiliation

Clemency = Forgiveness

Denizen = Inhabitant

Desiccate = To dry out

Dubious = Uncertain

Enigma = Mystery

Eradicate = Destroy

Expunge = Remove

Feign = Pretend

Flaunt = To show off

Florid = Red

Hirsute = Hairy

Illicit = Illegal

Inane = Silly

Indigent = Poor

Lucid = Clear

Moniker = Nickname

Phobia = Fear

Placid = Peaceful

Prosaic = Dull

Query = Question

Rectify = Correct

Rescind = To take back

E State Capitals

Alabama	Montgomery
Alaska	Juneau
Arizona	Phoenix
Arkansas	Little Rock
California	Sacramento
Colorado	Denver
Connecticut	Hartford
Delaware	Dover
Florida	Tallahassee
Georgia	Atlanta
Hawaii	Honolulu
Idaho	Boise
Illinois	Springfield
Indiana	Indianapolis
Iowa	Des Moines
Kansas	Topeka
Kentucky	Frankfort
Louisiana	Baton Rouge
Maine	Augusta
Maryland	Annapolis
Massachusetts	Boston
Michigan	Lansing
Minnesota	Saint Paul
Mississippi	Jackson
Missouri	Jefferson City
Montana	Helena
Nebraska	Lincoln
Nevada	Carson City
New Hampshire	Concord
New Jersey	Trenton
New Mexico	Santa Fe
New York	Albany

North Carolina	Raleigh
North Dakota	Bismarck
Ohio	Columbus
Oklahoma	Oklahoma City
Oregon	Salem
Pennsylvania	Harrisburg
Rhode Island	Providence
South Carolina	Columbia
South Dakota	Pierre
Tennessee	Nashville
Texas	Austin
Utah	Salt Lake City
Vermont	Montpelier
Virginia	Richmond
Washington	Olympia
West Virginia	Charleston
Wisconsin	Madison
Wyoming	Cheyenne

F Literature, Science, and Social Studies Lessons

Literature

Lower Level Passage

An Eskimo boy named Kuk went hunting for seals one winter. Seal hunting was done at sea, on top of the winter's thick layer of ice. Hunters would wait for the seals to come up through holes in the ice, and then shoot the seals before they could get back into the water. Before he left his village, Kuk packed his dogsled with enough supplies for a week. The first day, he traveled for a long time until his dogs had pulled him and his sled far out onto the sea.

After he set up camp that night, Kuk fed his sled dogs and then went to sleep early. It had been a long day and he was tired. During the night Kuk heard the sea ice making cracking and crunching sounds. But he went back to sleep without worry, because the ice was always making noises. When Kuk crawled out of his tent in the morning, he was surprised to discover that he was on a floating chunk of ice surrounded by water. His sled and supplies were nowhere in sight. Only his lead dog, Kanute, was on the ice chunk with him.

After three days and nights of floating on the ice chunk, Kuk couldn't stand the hunger any longer. He was becoming weak and was afraid of dying. He decided he would kill his dog and eat him. As he sat on the ice, Kuk pulled out his hunting knife and called his big dog to him. Kanute had a look of fear in his eyes but slowly walked towards Kuk. At the last second, Kuk got a sick feeling in his stomach and threw the knife onto the ice. He lay on the ice and cried.

As Kuk lay there, he realized that Kanute had circled around and was standing behind him, with his sharp teeth just inches from Kuk's neck. Kuk panicked as he realized that Kanute was also starving and now was probably going to kill him for food. Then he felt the dog's hot tongue licking his face and he began to cry.

The next day a search plane spotted two dark objects on a floating chunk of ice. The pontoon plane landed on the water. The pilot was able to rescue the boy and the dog, who were both too weak to move.

Upper Level Passage

There have been several stories, books, and movies about people trapped on deserted islands. One of the most famous books is *Robinson Crusoe.* This 300-year old novel was based on the real-life experiences of a Scottish sailor named Alexander Selkirk. Here is Selkirk's story.

Selkirk got into a dispute with his ship's captain as they were sailing through the Pacific Ocean. When the captain could no longer tolerate Selkirk's complaining and arguing, he put him ashore on a small deserted island. As the men in the rowboat were leaving, Selkirk begged to be taken back to the ship, but the captain refused. However, the captain was kind enough to give Selkirk some survival gear, which included a gun, knife, hatchet, blankets, and clothing.

Selkirk built himself a small hut with a grass covered roof. His survival depended mainly on the wild goats on the island. Goats were his main source of food, in addition to the crawfish. He also used goat hides for clothing and the walls of his shelter. Selkirk hunted the goats with his gun until his bullets ran out. After that he chased them on foot until he caught them. One day during a chase, he and a goat fell over the edge of a cliff. When he came to, the goat was lying dead underneath him.

The hardest thing for Selkirk was the loneliness. In the fictional novel, Robinson Crusoe met a man on the island who became his companion, but in real life, Selkirk was completely alone on the island. At night he would fall asleep while watching the sea, hoping for a ship to return. But Selkirk was tough enough to survive the loneliness without going crazy. Four years after being dropped off, some sailors rescued Selkirk. He returned to sailing and to living a normal life.

Science

Lower Level Passage

Different parts of the earth have different types of plants and animals. The temperature (how warm or cold it is) and the amount of rain are two things that determine the types of plants and animals. Based on temperature and rainfall, the earth can be divided into four parts.

One part of the Earth is called *tundra*. It is in the far northern part of the Earth, where it is cold most of the year. Only grasses, mosses, and small bushes grow in the tundra. There are no trees. Reindeer are the biggest animals that live on the tundra. Many types of birds also live on the tundra, especially during the short summers.

In the warmest parts of the Earth, where it rains a lot, there are tropical rain forests. Here it is hot and rainy almost every day. Many types of plants grow in the tropical rain forest, and many of them grow to be very large. There is also a large variety of animal life. Compared to the tundra, you will find more varieties of insects and cold-blooded animals like snakes and frogs.

Warm parts of the Earth that receive very little rain are deserts. Instead of soft grasses and leafy trees, most desert plants are prickly and have few leaves. For example, a cactus is a plant that grows well in a desert. The animals that live in a desert are usually small animals, such as lizards and rabbits that can live without much water.

Other parts of the Earth are made up of temperate forests. These regions have four seasons each year. Many varieties of trees grow in the temperate forests. They all lose their leaves in the fall, except for the evergreen trees. There are many varieties of mammals living in the temperate forests. They all grow thicker fur to stay warm when winter comes.

Upper Level Passage

There are several glands in the human body that control the rate of many bodily activities. A gland is a special organ that makes and releases chemicals called hormones. The blood transports these hormones to the body's organs that use them. The amount of hormones produced determines the activity level of the organs that depend on them. People can have serious health problems when glands do not produce the correct level of hormones.

The pituitary gland, which is about the size of a marble, is located at the base of the brain. This gland produces several hormones, the most important of which is the growth hormone. If there's too much growth hormone, a person's bones will grow very long. If there's too little growth hormone, bones will be very short.

The thyroid gland is located in the throat. The hormone it produces controls metabolism, the rate at which cells use food. If the thyroid produces too much hormone, cells will consume food rapidly. In such a case, a person may eat a lot and still lose weight. To function well, the thyroid requires enough iodine. That's why iodine is often added to the salt that people eat.

Another important gland is the adrenal gland. There are actually two of them, one on top of each kidney. Part of the adrenal glands' job is to create quick changes in the body. For example, when a person senses danger, the adrenals will immediately release a special hormone that makes the heart beat faster so that the person could immediately run if necessary. Another function of the adrenal glands is to maintain the body's water balance.

The pancreas, which is located behind the stomach, secretes a digestive hormone that controls the amount of food that is converted into glucose, a type of sugar. The blood delivers glucose to cells throughout the body that depend on glucose for energy. The pancreas also produces insulin, which determines how much glucose body cells are allowed to use. When the pancreas does not produce enough insulin, people have a disease called diabetes. People with diabetes depend on insulin shots so that their cells can get enough glucose.

Social Studies

Lower Level Passage

The Egyptians built great pyramids in which they buried their kings. Thousands of years after they died, you can see the bodies of these kings in museums. Their bodies still exist because they were made into mummies. Mummies are bodies that did not decay, because they were treated with special salts that dried out the bodies. The bodies were then carefully wrapped in linens, placed in coffins, and put into the pyramids or other secret places.

The Egyptians also mummified lots of pets and even wild animals before they buried them. The list includes cats, cows, dogs, birds, monkeys, and many more. Even elephant and lion mummies have been found. Sometimes, pets were made into mummies so that they could be with the king in the afterlife. Sometimes, the animals were made into mummies so that the king would have meat to eat in the afterlife. And other times, the animals were made into mummies because the Egyptians liked and respected those animals.

The Egyptians must have really liked cats. Hundreds of thousands of mummified cats have been found buried in one gigantic cat grave in the desert. Cat mummies have been found in at least eight other locations in Egypt. The mummies of special cats were placed inside wood carvings of cats.

Sometimes animals were made into mummies because they were thought to be gods. The Egyptian kings and priests always took care of a special bull that was thought to be a god. When he lived, the bull even wore gold and jewels. When he died, it took 110 days to make the body into a mummy. Then the mummified bull was carried through the streets filled with people and buried in a special place. Some other animals that were treated like gods during and after their lives include goats and crocodiles.

Today, scientists study the remains of the mummified animals to learn more about life in ancient Egypt. They have learned how the bodies were made into mummies, which animals the Egyptians worshipped, and what kinds of meat the Egyptians ate. They have also learned that people who did not own their own animals would buy animal mummies.

Upper Level Passage

Greenland is a large country that has a very small population. It also has an unlikely name, because there's nothing "green" about Greenland. In fact, Greenland is mostly white. Eighty percent of Greenland lies buried under snow and ice that is as much as two miles thick. This amounts to so much ice that if it all melted, sea levels around the world would rise by 24 feet.

Because of global warming, Greenland's glaciers are melting much faster than they ever have before. But even at the current rate, it would take hundreds of years for all the ice to melt. As the temperatures rise, Greenland is growing more food than it ever has before. The melting ice is also exposing minerals for mining and making it possible to drill for oil. Greenlanders are excited about the future of their warmer country.

The first European settlers to arrive in Greenland were Vikings from Iceland in the year 982. They were led by Erik the Red. They built churches and farms on which they raised sheep. They also hunted seals and purchased sealskins and walrus ivory from the natives. After about 400 years, all of the Vikings in Greenland disappeared. No one knows why, but it may have been because Greenland became much colder.

Today there are 56,000 people living in Greenland. Although Greenland is a fairly independent country, it is still officially ruled by the country of Denmark. Greenlanders live on rocky shorelines between the glaciers and the sea. There are no roads in Greenland; everyone has to travel by dogsled, water, or air. The lack of land transportation probably doesn't matter too much. Greenlanders have always made much of their living from the sea.

APPENDIX G Words for Grouping by Category

The words below can be categorized as transportation, musical instruments, house parts, birds, or mammals. There are six of each.

Penguin	Ship	Window
Moose	Crow	Piano
Door	Beaver	Skateboard
Flute	Taxi	Flamingo
Groundhog	Guitar	Bear
Airplane	Turkey	Recorder
Ostrich	Bicycle	Basement
Drums	Deck	Elephant
Chicken	Boat	Pig
Chimney	Violin	Steps

The words below can be categorized as games, plants, drinks, professions, or weather-related. There are six of each.

Clouds	Dancer	Lemonade
Banker	Hurricane	Corn
Wind	Roses	Soccer
Chess	Wine	Plumber
Snow	Tag	Forecast
Tobacco	Coffee	Geologist
Poker	Water	Cotton
Weeds	Peanuts	Temperature
Milkshake	Dentist	Volleyball
Carpenter	Uno	Juice

Shopping Lists

Directions

Use only one list at a time.

List A	List B	List C
Lettuce	Tomatoes	Cherries
Socks	Pants	Gloves
Helmet	Knife	Hammer
Goldfish	Paper	Folders
Bananas	Beans	Peanuts
Napkins	Cups	Battery
Soap	Toothpaste	Shampoo
Cards	Cap	Pencils
Turkey	Coke	Vitamins
Purse	T-shirt	Rug

List D	List E	List F
Coffee	Milk	Juice
Lotion	Pillow	Suitcase
Nails	Glue	Skateboard
Macaroni	Hot dogs	Ice cream
Newspaper	Lamp	Salt
Shovel	Water	Cell phone
Candy	Rice	Bread
Roses	Perfume	Kitten
Pajamas	Shirt	Boots
Grapes	Cookies	Plates

Visual–Spatial Grids

Examples of Shorthand and Abbreviations

And = &	Are = e
Because = bc	Before = b4
Between = in	But = b
Direction = dir	Equals = eq
Every = e	Everything = et
For = f	Has/have = h
Important = por	In = i
Memory = mem	Necessary = ns
Need = n	Nobody = nb
Nothing = nn	Number = no.
On = o	Opposite = op
Period = pe	Science = sy
Social studies = ss	Somebody = sb
Something = st	Student = stu
Teacher = te	The = l
They = g	Thing = t
This = c	Was = y
With = w	You = v

K   Pre- and Post-Tests

Auditory Short–Term Memory Span Pre-Test

Student's Name _____ Grade _____ Date _____

Directions

Administer these items before beginning the training program. Read the words at the rate of one word per second, and let your voice drop on the last word. Do *not* repeat any items if the student asks for a repeat. In order for an item to be scored as correct, all of the words for that item must be repeated in exactly the same order. Regardless of the student's age or ability, begin with the first item. Stop when there have been four consecutive incorrect responses. Then determine the longest correct response and record it at the bottom of this sheet. The length of that response is the student's auditory short-term memory span. For example, if the student's highest level correct item is four words in length, then the student's span is four. A normal span is three to five words for elementary students and five to seven words for adolescents.

Read these directions to the student and then proceed with the items:

I'm going to say some words. When I am finished, you say the words in the same order that I said them. We will begin with two words.

Items

Mark a C for correct in front of correct items and an I for incorrect in front of the incorrect items.

  ___ Meat—Pride

  ___ Steam—Truth

  ___ Grief—Bloom—Air

  ___ Love—Wheat—Cat

  ___ Shore—Thief—Joke—Boy

  ___ Tool—Mood—Square—Lip

  ___ Plant—Vest—Hall—Goose—In

  ___ Dove—Golf—Think—Warm—Pack

  ___ Fight—Rock—Doll—Mind—Lake—Month

  ___ Snake—Dream—Boss—Earth—Book—Horse

  ___ Peach—Law—Table—Plain—Monk—Dirt—Charm

  ___ Code—Dress—Soap—Bowl—Storm—Brain—Church

  ___ Girl—Judge—Shame—Thin—Lump—Truck—Pipe—Door

  ___ Ship—Greed—Moss—Form—Woods—Price—Birds—Crime

Student's pre-test auditory short-term memory span: _____

Auditory Short–Term Memory Span Post–Test

Student's Name _____   Grade _____   Date _____

Directions

Administer these items after completion of the training program. Read the words at the rate of one word per second, and let your voice drop on the last word. Do *not* repeat any items if the student asks for a repeat. In order for an item to be scored as correct, all of the words for that item must be repeated in exactly the same order. Regardless of the student's age or ability, begin with the first item. Stop when there have been four consecutive incorrect responses. Then determine the longest correct response and record it at the bottom of this sheet. The length of that response is the student's auditory short-term memory span. For example, if the student's highest level correct item is four words in length, then the student's span is four. A normal span is three to five words for elementary students and five to seven words for adolescents.

Read these directions to the student and then proceed with the items:

I'm going to say some words. When I am finished, you say the words in the same order that I said them. We will begin with two words.

Items

Mark a C for correct in front of correct items and an I for incorrect in front of the incorrect items.

___ Fork—Kiss

___ Board—Hope

___ Table—Gift—Toast

___ Green—Branch—Dog

___ Pop—World—Hour—Moss

___ Dock—Poet—Shock—Dress

___ Cost—Speech—Wife—Blood—Sole

___ Wine—Claw—Troops—Child—Brute

___ Hoof—Mast—Oats—House—Yacht—Fire

___ Star—Truce—Couch—Learn—Queen—Rock

___ Lump—Chair—Pact—Cord—Stent—Greed—Foul

___ Bird—Sauce—Priest—Hint—Crash—Strong—Tool

___ Beast—Square—Iron—Time—Death—Plank—Cane—Pray

___ Tank—Suds—Mule—Wrench—Plant—Thorn—Gem—Flood

Student's *post-test* auditory short-term memory span: _____

Student's *pre-test* auditory short-term memory span: _____

Change in student's auditory short-term memory span: _____

Verbal Delayed Recall Pre-Test

Student's Name _____ Grade _____ Date _____

Directions

Administer these items before beginning the training program. Read the same list of items four times in order to give the student an opportunity to learn them. Read the list more slowly than the auditory short-term memory span list, pausing for one second between words so that the rate is two seconds per word. Allow the student to respond after each reading of the list, and check the words the student recalls correctly. The words can be recalled in any order. In the appropriate *trial* column, check each word the student recalls. The number of words the student recalls after the fourth trial is the number of words the student has learned. After a delay of approximately 20 minutes, ask the student to recall the words again, and check those recalled under the *delayed* column heading. The number of words recalled at this time is the student's level of verbal delayed recall.

Before reading the items the first time, say:

I am going to read you a list of shopping items four different times. Try to learn as many as you can. After I read the list each time, I will ask you to remember as many as you can. I also will ask you to remember them again 20 minutes from now. You do *not* need to remember them in order.

When finished reading the list, say:

Now tell me as many items as you can remember. They can be in any order.

After the student has responded, proceed with trials 2 to 4. At the beginning of each trial, say:

I am going to read the same shopping list again. Try to remember as many as you can.

Each time you finish reading the list, say:

Now tell me as many items as you can remember. They can be in any order.

Items

| | Trials | | | | |
Items	First	Second	Third	Fourth	Delayed
Gloves					
Chair					
Toothpaste					
Cherries					
Desk					
Belt					
Peaches					
Socks					
Lamp					
Oranges					
Hairbrush					
Bed					
Lotion					
Perfume					
Dress					
Bananas					
Shampoo					
Pants					
Shelf					
Raisins					

Number of items recalled after fourth trial: _____

Number of items recalled after a 20-minute delay: _____

Verbal Delayed Recall Post–Test

Student's Name _____ Grade _____ Date _____

Directions

Administer these items after completion of the training program. Read the same list of items four times in order to give the student an opportunity to learn them. Read the list more slowly than the auditory short-term memory span list, pausing for one second between words so that the rate is two seconds per word. Allow the student to respond after each reading of the list, and check the words the student recalls correctly. The words can be recalled in any order. In the appropriate *trial* column, check each word the student recalls. The number of words the student recalls after the fourth trial is the number of words the student has learned. After a delay of approximately 20 minutes, ask the student to recall the words again, and check those recalled under the *delayed* column heading. The number of words recalled at this time is the student's level of verbal delayed recall.

Before reading the items the first time, say:

I am going to read you a list of shopping items four different times. Try to learn as many as you can. After I read the list each time, I will ask you to remember as many as you can. I also will ask you to remember them again 20 minutes from now. You do *not* need to remember them in order.

When finished reading the list, say:

Now tell me as many items as you can remember. They can be in any order.

After the student has responded, proceed with trials 2 to 4. At the beginning of each trial, say:

I am going to read the same shopping list again. Try to remember as many as you can.

Each time you finish reading the list, say:

Now tell me as many items as you can remember. They can be in any order.

Items

Trials

Items	First	Second	Third	Fourth	Delayed
Pillows					
Baseball					
Erasers					
Carrots					
Golf club					
Dresser					
Beans					
Folders					
Skates					
Couch					
Potatoes					
Crayons					
Table					
Frisbee					
Notebook					
Lettuce					
Jump rope					
Rug					
Onions					
Backpack					

Post-Test number of items recalled after fourth trial: _____

Pre-Test number of items recalled after fourth trial: _____

Change in number of items recalled after the fourth trial: _____

Post-Test number of items recalled after a 20-minute delay: _____

Pre-Test number of items recalled after a 20-minute delay: _____

Change in number of items recalled after a 20-minute delay: _____

Review Sheet

Review Sheet

Name _____ Subject/Topic _____

Dates Reviewed ____ ____ ____ ____ ____

Page Number	Question	Answer	Correct Responses					

APPENDIX M

Parent Instructions for Working Memory Exercises

Parent Directions for Using Arithmetic to Build Memory (Lesson 19)

Arithmetic flashcards facts can be used to strengthen your child's short-term and working memory.

Here are the details:

1. Use arithmetic facts that your child already knows well. They can be addition, subtraction, multiplication, or division facts, as long as the child knows most of the answers almost immediately.
2. Mix the cards up each time you use them.
3. Show the child the first card and wait for the child to say the answer. For example, if the card shows 5 + 2, wait for the child to say "seven". If the child makes a mistake, immediately say the correct answer.
4. Then remove the flashcard from view and place it behind an object so that you can see it but the child can't.
5. Then do the same with the next flashcard in the deck and continue showing the child new flashcards until you reach the level the child is at. (Your child's memory trainer will tell which level to work at.)
6. When you reach the level the child is at, stop showing new cards and ask the child to tell you the answers to the math facts in the same order that they were shown. For example, if the child was shown 5 + 2, then 4 + 5, and then 7 + 1, the child should say "seven, nine, eight".
7. Whether or not the child remembers the answers in the correct sequence, do another set of cards in the same manner and at the same level.
8. Practice this for at least 10 minutes per day, at least three days per week.
9. When the child successfully completes 10 sets in a row at least five different times, you can try the next level. For example, when the child has successfully mastered remembering a sequence of two answers, you can require the child to remember three answers in a row.
10. Tell the child's memory trainer when the child advances to the next level so that the trainer practices with the child at the same level.

Parent Directions for Using Playing Cards to Build Memory (Lesson 20)

A deck of regular playing cards can be used to strengthen your child's short-term and working memory. To play, the child must remember cards he or she has seen a certain number of cards back. For example, it works like this when the child must remember what he or she saw two cards back: if the child sees 6–3–4–7–5 one at a time, he or she should say "six" when the 4 is shown, "three" when the 7 is shown, and "four" when the 5 is shown, and so on.

Here are the details:

1. Shuffle a deck of cards.
2. Show the child the first card for 1 to 2 seconds.
3. Then remove it from view and place it behind an object so that you can see it but the child can't.
4. Then show the child the next card for 1 to 2 seconds and remove it from view and place it alongside the other hidden card so that you can always see the sequence of the cards.
5. Once you reach the level where the child must begin responding (your child's memory trainer will tell which level to work at), say "now" after you show a new card. The child is then to say what he or she saw a certain number of cards ago. After the child says the name of the card, allow him or her 1 second to view the new card and then remove it and place it with the others.
6. Then as you show each new card, the child should immediately name the next card he or she previously saw in the sequence.
7. Continue showing new cards until the child makes a mistake. Stop as soon as a mistake is made and start the process all over again.
8. The goal is to have the child correctly remember a sequence of 10 cards. When this is accomplished, start over with a new sequence. When the child successfully completes 10 in a row at least five different times, you can try the next level. For example, when the child can successfully remember the sequence two cards back, you can try three cards back.
9. Practice this for at least 10 minutes per day, at least three days per week.
10. Tell the child's memory trainer when the child advances to the next level so that the trainer practices with the child at the same level.

References

Alloway, T. P., & Gathercole, S. E. (Eds.). (2006). *Working memory and neurodevelopmental disorders*. New York, NY: Psychology Press.

Baddeley, A. D. (1986). *Working memory*. Oxford, UK: Oxford University Press.

Baddeley, A. D., Eysenck, M. W., & Anderson, M. C. (2009). *Memory*. New York, NY: Psychology Press.

Cohen, G., & Conway, M. A. (Eds.). (2008). *Memory in the real world*. New York, NY: Psychology Press.

Dehn, M. J. (2008). *Working memory and academic learning: Assessment and intervention*. Hoboken, NJ: Wiley.

Dehn, M. J. (2010). *Long-term memory problems in children and adolescents: Assessment, intervention, and effective instruction*. Hoboken, NJ: Wiley.

Doidge, N. (2007). *The brain that changes itself*. New York, NY: Viking.

Emilien, G., Durlach, C., Antoniadis, E., Van Der Linden, M., & Maloteaux, J-M. (2004). *Memory: Neuropsychological, imaging, and psychopharmacological perspectives*. New York, NY: Psychology Press.

Gathercole, S. E., & Alloway, T. P. (2008). *Working memory and learning: A practical guide for teachers*. Los Angeles, CA: Sage.

Grilli, M. D., & Glisky, E. L. (2010). Self-imaging enhances recognition memory in memory-impaired individuals with neurological damage. *Neuropsychology, 24*, 698–710.

Klingberg, T. (2009). *The overflowing brain: Information overload and the limits of working memory*. New York, NY: Oxford University Press.

Oakes, L. M., & Bauer, P. J. (Eds.). (2007). *Short- and long-term memory in infancy and early childhood*. Oxford, UK: Oxford University Press.

Schacter, D. L. (1996). *Searching for memory*. New York, NY: Basic Books.

Schneider, W. (2010). Metacognition and memory development in childhood and adolescence. In H. S. Waters & W. Schneider (Eds.), *Metacognition, strategy use, and instruction* (pp. 54–84). New York, NY: Guilford Press.

Squire, L. R., & Schacter, D. L. (Eds.). (2002). *Neuropsychology of memory*. New York, NY: Guilford Press.

Tulving, E., & Craik, F. I. M. (Eds.). (2000). *The Oxford handbook of memory*. Oxford, UK: Oxford University Press.

Wilson, B. A. (2009). *Memory rehabilitation: Integrating theory and practice*. New York, NY: Guilford Press.

Worthen, J. B., & Hunt, R. R. (2011). *Mnemonology: Mnemonics for the 21st century*. New York, NY: Psychology Press.

About the CD-ROM

Introduction

This appendix provides you with the information on the contents of the CD that accompanies this book. For the latest and greatest information, please refer to the ReadMe file located at the root of the CD.

System Requirements

➤ A computer with a processor running at 120 Mhz or faster
➤ At least 32 MB of total RAM installed on your computer; for best performance, we recommend at least 64MB
➤ A CD-ROM drive

Note: Many popular word processing programs are capable of reading Microsoft Word files. However, users should be aware that a slight amount of formatting might be lost when using a program other than Microsoft Word.

Using the CD with Windows

To install the items from the CD to your hard drive, follow these steps:

1. Insert the CD into your computer's CD-ROM drive.
2. The CD-ROM interface will appear. The interface provides a simple point-and-click way to explore the contents of the CD.

If the opening screen of the CD-ROM does not appear automatically, follow these steps to access the CD:

1. Click the Start button on the left of the taskbar and then choose Run from the menu that pops up. (In Windows Vista and Windows 7, skip this step.)
2. In the dialog box that appears, type d:\setup.exe. (If your CD drive is not drive *D*, use the appropriate letter in place of *D*.) This brings up the CD interface described in the preceding set of steps. (In Windows Vista or Windows 7, type d:\setup.exe in the Start > Search text box.)

Using the CD with a Mac

1. Insert the CD into your computer's CD-ROM drive.
2. The CD-ROM icon appears on your desktop, double-click the icon.

3. Double-click the Start icon.

4. The CD-ROM interface will appear. The interface provides a simple point-and-click way to explore the contents of the CD.

What's on the CD

The following sections provide a summary of the software and other materials you'll find on the CD.

Content

This companion CD-ROM contains copies of 81 lessons and 11 appendixes from the book in Word (.doc) format. They can be customized, printed out, and distributed All documentation is included in the folder named "Content."

Applications

The following applications are on the CD:

OpenOffice.org

OpenOffice.org is a free multi-platform office productivity suite. It is similar to Microsoft Office or Lotus SmartSuite, but OpenOffice.org is absolutely free. It includes word processing, spreadsheet, presentation, and drawing applications that enable you to create professional documents, newsletters, reports, and presentations. It supports most file formats of other office software. You should be able to edit and view any files created with other office solutions. Certain features of Microsoft Word documents may not display as expected from within OpenOffice.org. For system requirements, go to www.openoffice.org.

Software can be of the following types:

➤ Shareware programs are fully functional, free, trial versions of copyrighted programs. If you like particular programs, register with their authors for a nominal fee and receive licenses, enhanced versions, and technical support.

➤ Freeware programs are free, copyrighted games, applications, and utilities. You can copy them to as many computers as you like—for free—but they offer no technical support.

➤ GNU software is governed by its own license, which is included inside the folder of the GNU software. There are no restrictions on distribution of GNU software. See the GNU license at the root of the CD for more details.

➤ Trial, demo, or evaluation versions of software are usually limited either by time or functionality (such as not letting you save a project after you create it).

Troubleshooting

If you have difficulty installing or using any of the materials on the companion CD, try the following solutions:

➤ **Turn off any antivirus software that you may have running.** Installers sometimes mimic virus activity and can make your computer incorrectly believe that a virus is infecting it. (Be sure to turn the antivirus software back on later.)

➤ **Close all running programs.** The more programs that you're running, the less memory is available to other programs. Installers also typically update files and programs; if you keep other programs running, installation may not work properly.

➤ **Reference the README file.** Please refer to the README file located at the root of the CD for the latest product information at the time of publication.

User Assistance

If you have trouble with the CD-ROM, please call the Wiley Product Technical Support phone number at (800) 762-2974. Outside the United States, call 1 (317) 572-3994. You can also contact Wiley Product Technical Support at **http://support.wiley.com.** John Wiley & Sons will provide technical support only for installation and other general quality control items. For technical support of the applications themselves, consult the program vendor or author.

To place additional orders or to request information about other Wiley products, please call (800) 225-5945.

Customer Note: If this Book is Accompanied by Software, Please Read the Following Before Opening the Package.

This software contains files to help you utilize the models described in the accompanying book. By opening the package, you are agreeing to be bound by the following agreement:

This software product is protected by copyright and all rights are reserved by the author, John Wiley & Sons, Inc., or their licensors. You are licensed to use this software on a single computer. Copying the software to another medium or format for use on a single computer does not violate the U.S. Copyright Law. Copying the software for any other purpose is a violation of the U.S. Copyright Law.

This software product is sold as is without warranty of any kind, either express or implied, including but not limited to the implied warranty of merchantability and fitness for a particular purpose. Neither Wiley nor its dealers or distributors assumes any liability for any alleged or actual damages arising from the use of or the inability to use this software. (Some states do not allow the exclusion of implied warranties, so the exclusion may not apply to you.)